INSTITUTE OF LEADERSHIP & MANAG

SUPER SERIES

Information in Management

FOURTH EDITION

Published for the
Institute of Leadership & Management by

Pergamon
Flexible
Learning

AMSTERDAM BOSTON HEIDELBERG LONDON NEW YORK OXFORD
PARIS SAN DIEGO SAN FRANCISCO SINGAPORE SYDNEY TOKYO

Pergamon Flexible Learning
An imprint of Elsevier
Linacre House, Jordan Hill, Oxford OX2 8DP
30 Corporate Drive, Burlington, MA 01803

First published 1986
Second edition 1991
Third edition 1997
Fourth edition 2003
Reprinted 2003, 2005

British Library Cataloguing in Publication Data
A catalogue record for this book is available from the British Library

ISBN 0 7506 5890 8

For information on Pergamon Flexible Learning
visit our website at www.bh.com/pergamonfl

Institute of Leadership & Management
registered office
1 Giltspur Street
London
EC1A 9DD
Telephone 020 7294 3053
www.i-l-m.com
ILM is part of the City & Guilds Group

Working together to grow
libraries in developing countries

www.elsevier.com | www.bookaid.org | www.sabre.org

ELSEVIER   BOOK AID
            International   Sabre Foundation

The views expressed in this work are those of the authors and do
not necessarily reflect those of the Institute of Leadership &
Management or of the publisher

Author: Bob Foley
Editor: Heather Serjeant
Partially based on previous material by Howard Senter, Ian Bloor and Peter Elliott
Editorial management: Genesys, www.genesys-consultants.com
Composition by Genesis Typesetting Limited, Rochester, Kent
Printed and bound in China

Contents

Contents

Workbook introduction

1 ILM Super Series study links

This workbook addresses the issues of *Information in Management*. Should you wish to extend your study to other Super Series workbooks covering related or different subject areas, you will find a comprehensive list at the back of this book.

2 Links to ILM Qualifications

This workbook relates to the following learning outcomes in segments from the ILM Level 3 Introductory Certificate in First Line Management and the Level 3 Certificate in First Line Management.

C10.2   Analysing Information
  1. Analyse numerical data to extract relevant information
  2. Use appropriate statistics to enhance understanding of information
  3. Interpret statistical information from tables, charts or diagrams to reach conclusions
  4. Analyse qualitative information

C10.3   Using Information for Decisions
  1. Understand the need to collect information relevant to the decision to be made
  2. Use a decision-making model for problem solving

C10.4 Presenting Information
1 Select the most appropriate way to present statistical information
2 Present charts and diagrams effectively
3 Explain the information in charts and diagrams to others

3 Links to S/NVQs in Management

This workbook relates to the following elements of the Management Standards which are used in S/NVQs in Management, as well as a range of other S/NVQs.

D1.1 Gather required information
D1.2 Inform and advise others

It will also help you develop the following Personal Competences:

- communicating;
- influencing others;
- searching for information;
- thinking and taking decisions.

4 Workbook objectives

In a sense we all start life without information and we generally spend most of our first two decades of life painfully amassing enough of it to have a fair chance of surviving on our own. A lot of this is trial and error. We don't come into the world *knowing* that falling off a chair will hurt: we have to discover it for ourselves.

Of course, a lot of what we learn comes from other people. They provide an example, and they also supply us with 'precepts' – information and instructions designed to help us avoid the worst kinds of mistakes. But basically, acquiring wisdom is about trial and error. We try things out, collect information about the experience, and try to do it better next time.

Managers also learn from experience, though they may prefer not to think of it as a process of trial and error. In the world of work, the stakes are often very high, and while we can learn a great deal from a wrong decision, employers have a strong preference for right ones. A wrong decision can mean a lost customer, an unnecessary conflict, a spoiled batch of product, lost time and money. Even a decision that isn't as right as it could be will attract criticism.

To make a good decision we need (a) information and (b) ways of analysing it. Of course we also need intelligence and good judgement, but not even the most experienced manager can be sure of making a good decision if the information isn't there.

Here is a simple equation that we should always bear in mind.

$$\text{information} \times \text{analysis} \times \text{experience} \ = \ \text{good decisions}$$

All managers are greedy consumers of information. They typically spend well over half of their working time receiving, exchanging or issuing information, and they receive three times as much information as they issue.

- That's why modern organizations place so much emphasis on systems that provide the right information to the right people at the right time.
- That's why information technology has grown so rapidly.
- That's why managers are increasingly expected to use information-handling technology and software.

That's also why this is called the 'information age', and why the role of the manager can be seen as processing information in order to achieve results.

In this workbook we will consider the practical uses of information in organizations from several angles. This includes the role of information in the decision-making process and some of the models used for decision-making. We introduce a variety of statistical techniques and demonstrate how software tools such as spreadsheets and spreadsheet databases can help to analyse data. Finally we look at various methods of presenting information to make it easier to understand, for example using tables, charts and diagrams, and to help with making decisions.

4.1 Objectives

At the end of this workbook you should be better able to:

■ understand the need to collect information relevant to decisions;
■ use decision-making models;
■ analyse numerical data;
■ use statistics to enhance understanding of information;
■ analyse qualitative information;
■ select the most appropriate way to present statistical information;
■ present charts and diagrams effectively;
■ interpret statistical information from tables, charts or diagrams;
■ use spreadsheets and spreadsheet databases.

5 Activity planner

The following Activities need some planning and you may want to look at them now.

■ Activity 4, which asks you to analyse a recent decision affecting your work in terms of the six typical decision-making stages.
■ Activity 12, where you use a spreadsheet to carry out 'what-if' analysis.
■ Activity 20, which asks you to demonstrate basic spreadsheet skills such as data and formula entry, formatting text and numbers, and encourages you to do all the remaining activities using a spreadsheet.
■ Activity 39 which asks you to develop a house style and a word processing template for your workteam's non-numerical documents and reports.
■ Activity 51, which asks you to create an organization chart for your workteam or department and a procedure flow chart for a routine work activity.

Some or all of these Activities may provide the basis of evidence for your S/NVQ portfolio. All Portfolio Activities and the Work-based assignment are sign posted with this icon.

The icon states the elements to which the Portfolio Activities and Work-based assignment relate.

6 A note about spreadsheets

There are a number of Activities and Examples in the text that require you to use a spreadsheet. These have been designed to be worked out using Microsoft Excel and the formulae given may not work on other spreadsheets. Please consult your spreadsheet user documentation.

Session A
Using information for decisions

1 Introduction

Making a decision implies that you have considered several courses of action, and then made a choice.

For instance, suppose it is 7 am and you have just woken up. You have the choice between getting up or dozing off again.

Activity 1

2 mins

What do you need to know to make this getting-up decision?

_____

_____

_____

_____

_____

- Are you still tired?
- Is the bed warm?
- Is the bedroom cold?
- What day is it?
- Where do you have to be later and how long will it take to get there?
- Will you have to make a bit of effort with your appearance for whatever you have to do today?
- Are you hungry or thirsty?

In other words, even for a simple decision you need lots of **information**.

In this case all the information is already stored in your head and the choices are simple Yes/No choices. Many day-to-day business decisions are pretty straightforward too – is the phone ringing? If yes, pick it up and deal with the caller. You don't need a book to tell you that!

This book is about more complicated uses of information. In this session, we'll think about what information is needed to help organizations function, how business decisions are made, and what tools and techniques are available to help you make better decisions.

2 Adequate and relevant information

2.1 Information in organizations

Organizations function because people provide each other with information and act on it.

Even in the biggest organization, the top executives need information from the lowest levels of operations, and the newest team member needs to know what his or her work is supposed to achieve. In between, there are layers of management responsibility in which everyone needs information relevant to his or her job.

This figure shows a simplified version of **how the information flows** around an organization.

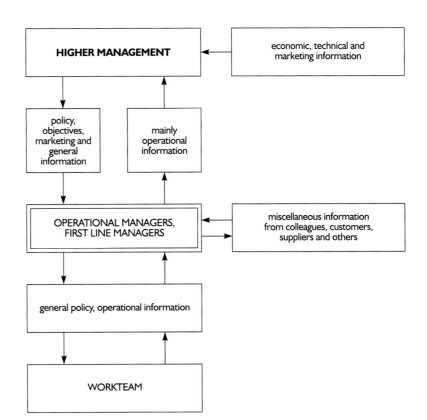

The information each group is given depends on its needs.

Activity 2 · 5 mins

Company Z, a financial services business, is organized into three departments selling mortgages, personal loans and savings plans respectively.

Activity levels, sales and cash flow are all-important, so departmental and section managers generate detailed information on these daily. They themselves receive weekly reports on all other operational matters, especially staff performance. There may be a considerable amount of information, including the detailed performance of individual sales staff on an hourly basis, if the system is capable of collecting this data.

Managers at all levels in Company Z need this information to ensure that the company's extremely tight business targets are met.

How much of this performance information does higher management need to receive?

_____

_____

What, if anything, do the workteam members need to be told?

_____

_____

Generally, the top managers (the senior executives) of an organization try to keep clear of operational details. They don't have time to wade through it, and it isn't their job anyway. It is the responsibility of operational management to deliver in key result areas.

What top management want is bottom-line information about key areas such as sales, revenue and cash flow. They will not be interested in operational matters and the detail of staff performance, productivity and so on unless they think there is a problem that may affect the bottom line.

Being in the financial services industry, Company Z is very sensitive to some external developments, especially the constantly moving exchange rates, bank interest rates and share prices. The internal financial information has to be measured against these external data. The two sets of data can be combined to provide instant updates to financial forecasts.

The workteams also need information. They are working under pressure to meet targets, and they need to know how they are doing. Most such organizations would probably give them feedback at least weekly.

Activity 3 · 3 mins

What value is there in providing workteams with information about performance?

_____

_____

It is a matter of motivating the workteam. People need to know what they are expected to achieve, and how well they are doing.

This could be done with large charts showing targets and actual performance. This information could help motivate them to better performance.

There are many multi-branch organizations where lots of geographically separate units are basically doing the same thing, for example estate agents, betting shops, retailers or tyre fitters. Here it is useful for both managers and workteams to be told how other units are performing. If District 9 can cut shrinkage to 3%, so can others. If the Glasgow branch can exceed its sales targets for the new product by 29%, then so can others.

Again, league tables and charts can help stimulate competitiveness and motivate people to greater efforts.

2.2 Decision-making

Whatever the management level, decision-making in an organization typically has six stages, each involving information.

1 Problem recognition

The decision maker needs to know that there is a problem in the first place, and normally further information is required.

■ **Quantitative information**: it is much easier to make decisions if they can be put in numerical terms: doing it this way will take five hours, whereas doing it that way will only take three; this will cost £2,000 whereas that will cost £1,750, and so on.
■ **Qualitative or intangible information**: it probably won't be possible to put all of the things affecting a decision into precise numbers, for example the effect on team spirit. Just because these things are not quantifiable doesn't mean they are not relevant to the decision.

2 Problem definition and structuring

Once you have further information you need to analyse it so that the problem can be defined more precisely.

For example, suppose your company has falling sales. The fall in overall sales revenue would alert you to the problem, but further information would be needed to identify exactly where the falls were occurring. If you discovered that sales of product A in the north region are falling and investigated this, the problem could perhaps be expressed as a question, as follows.

'Decline of sales of product A in north region, due to new competitor: how can the decline be reversed?'

Unfortunately, many problems will be more vague than this. There are a number of ways of defining and structuring a problem, for exmple:

■ as a mathematical model;
■ as a scenario in 'what-if?' analysis (probably using a spreadsheet);
■ using a decision tree.

3 Identifying alternative courses of action

Usually a problem will have a number of possible solutions, and once the alternative courses of action are identified, more information is needed about each of them so they can be assessed.

Suppose your company wants to review the price of product A in the north region: information will be needed about the effect of particular price levels on demand for the product.

Such information can include external information such as market research (demand at a particular price) and internal information such as the cost of the product and how it could be reduced. Once again, in this kind of decision it may be useful to use modelling techniques.

4 Making and communicating the decision

The decision will be made after weighing up the information about each of the alternative solutions. (Note that a choice *not* to do something is still a decision.)

A decision is useless if nobody knows about it. You may decide to lower the price of product A and run an intensive advertising campaign in the north region, but nothing will happen unless the packaging is changed and the advertising department is informed. That may seem obvious, but it is all too common for decisions taken in one part of an organization to come as a complete surprise to others who needed to know!

5 Implementing the decision

The decision is then put into action or implemented. Implementation involves lots of planning and review. Information is needed to make sure that everything is going according to plan.

6 Review of the effects of the decision

After a decision has been made and implemented, yet more information is needed about how well it worked. If it doesn't achieve the desired effects, more decisions will be needed. Whether or not it achieves the desired effects, managers can add this whole decision-making process to their experience and make faster, better (and better-informed) decisions in the future.

Activity 4

10 mins

S/NVQ D1.1

This Activity may provide the basis of appropriate evidence for your S/NVQ portfolio. If you are intending to take this copurse of action, it might be better to write your answers on separate sheets of paper.

Think of a fairly major new decision affecting the work of your workteam that has been taken and implemented while you have worked there. See if you can analyse it in terms of the six decision-making stages. What gave rise to the decision in the first place? What were the choices? What information was needed to help make the decision and what tools and techniques were used to analyse the information? Did it have the desired effect?

2.3 Effective decision-making

So managers need information to help them throughout the decision-making process.

Decisions made without information are risky. Experience can sometimes make them less risky, because it means knowing what usually happens in a particular situation. Unfortunately, this isn't always enough.

Activity 5

Ashlar Accessories Ltd received a faxed order from a customer for 25 laser printer toner cartridges. The customer service clerk couldn't make out the fax clearly and wasn't sure whether the order stated Series 4 or Series 5 machines. He took the order to the section manager, who looked briefly at the order and told him to send Series 4 cartridges. 'That could be a four', she said. 'Anyway, they've always had Series 4 in the past, so that's probably what they want this time'.

The section manager's decision is based on past experience of this customer, and probably she is right.

Would you make the same decision? _____

If not, what would you have done?

_____

_____

This is not a trivial matter. Laser toner cartridges are quite expensive items, and this order may have a total ex-VAT value of over £1,000. It will also be fairly bulky, so there will be a significant delivery cost. It would pay to make sure the order was right.

Even if the order was small, there is customer satisfaction to consider. Customers do not like receiving the wrong goods, even if it is their own fault! An experienced manager should have known that it pays to check.

What was the information on which the section manager based her decision?

- First, there was information which was correct, but referred to past experience: this customer had previously ordered Series 4 cartridges. However, what was right in the past may be wrong now. Perhaps the customer has upgraded to Series 5 machines.
- Second, there was information that was uncertain – the hard-to-read fax message.

Either of these presents a problem: information that is old, uncertain, or perhaps incomplete, can lead to wrong decisions being made. And where money, time and customer service are involved, it pays to be certain. A simple phone call would have removed all doubt.

2.4 Costs and benefits of seeking information

In practice, managers rarely have all the information they might like when making decisions. But is it always worth the effort and cost of obtaining more? Let's look at a couple of ways a manager might decide.

Activity 6

5 mins

Rashid was due to give a presentation on the other side of town. Just as he was about to leave, he remembered that there was no spare bulb for the overhead projector He ran down to the technical department and asked for a spare. 'What model is it?', they asked, but Rashid couldn't remember. 'Oh well – you'd better take one of these', they said. 'It fits most types so it should be OK.'

What considerations would you weigh up when making a decision of this kind?

_____

_____

Rashid is in a hurry, so he has to weigh up two quite complex options.

- **Option 1: go and get reliable information.** This will take time, and there will be a risk of being late for the presentation.
- **Option 2: take a bulb which may not work.** The risk here is that if the original bulb fails, the replacement may not work, and the presentation will be ruined.

Rashid can only choose one option, so in each case he needs to consider two separate factors that will contribute to the 'risk score' and allocate a value to each in regard to:

- the probability of the risk becoming a reality (say 50% in the case of option 1);
- the seriousness of this on a scale of 1 to 100 (say 40 out of 100, or 40% for option 1).

He then needs to multiply the two factors together, which in this case gives us a final risk score of $50 \times 40 = 20\%$. This means that there is a one-in-five chance of a bad outcome for option 1.

In option 2, the risk of the original bulb failing is about 1 in 20 or 5%, and the risk of the spare not working is 1 in 4 or 25%. This gives a total risk of $5 \times 25 = 1.25\%$. The seriousness of this happening quite high, say 80%, but the risk score still works out quite low: $1.25 \times 80 = 1\%$ or a one in a hundred chance of a bad outcome for option 2.

In this case, then, it is not worth Rashid's while to get accurate information, because the cost of the time taken to do so produces a higher risk score.

Of course, Rashid did not really have time to sit down and work his decision out on paper. But there is often a case for doing so, when the stakes are high.

Another way to evaluate whether it is worth getting accurate information is to balance out the pros and cons, or positive and negative factors, using your judgement to rate each factor out of 10. Here is an example.

	Decision A	Decision B
Positive factors		
Cost/value	+ 8	+ 5
Importance	+ 7	+ 6
Negative factors		
Pressure of time	− 6	− 8
Cost/time required to obtain fuller information	− 5	− 6
Total score	+ 4	− 3

A positive number means it is worth taking the time and effort to get more and better information. A negative figure means it isn't.

2.5 How much information?

If you have too little information, you cannot reach a good-quality decision. You need to acquire more information – but how much?

For example, suppose a first line manager named Ronald was trying to decide which of three different specifications for fire extinguishers would be most appropriate for his office, which contained a lot of electrical equipment. He read through the manufacturers' literature but wasn't sure. Did it tell him everything he wanted to know? He called the local Fire Prevention Department for advice. They faxed him some further documents. Still Ronald felt uncertain. He wrote back to the manufacturers asking some technical questions and asked one of his team to search the Internet for any relevant articles.

He contacted the British Standards Institution, the Department of Trade and Industry, the Fire Protection Association and his company's insurers, all of whom sent him more information. Finally, he got hold of some obscure research reports, which he found very hard to understand. In the end, he spent more than two whole days studying the information before he made his decision.

Choosing the right fire extinguishers is an important decision, and it is vital to have reliable information. But, as we have seen, information has a cost to set against its value:

- it may have to be paid for;
- it takes time to locate and acquire;
- it takes time to read and understand.

If Ronald earns £20,000 a year, with additional costs taking his total cost to his employer to around £40,000, that works out at over £160 per working day. If it has taken him more than two days to study the fire extinguisher issue, the cost of his time alone is probably over £320. To this must be added the time of the other team member involved, other colleagues, phone calls, postage, and so on.

Then we have to consider the cost of the things Ronald could have been doing in that time – perhaps more important and valuable tasks.

Was Ronald spending his time cost-effectively?

Activity 7 · 4 mins

Here are three graphs that show the cost of getting additional information and its value in making decisions. Which of the three graphs describes Ronald's case?

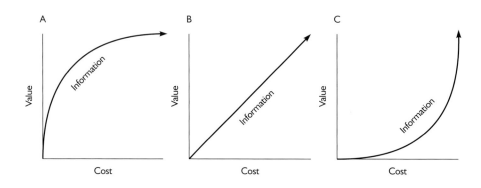

Comment briefly on what the graph means.

_____

_____

_____

The answers to this Activity can be found on page 128.

Actually, the situation is usually worse than this. As more information piles up, it becomes harder and harder to manage it. Information overload makes it more difficult to make quality decisions, so our cost/value graph might end up looking like this.

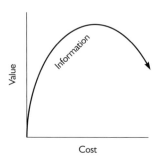

Like so many things, the cost-value curve for information tends to follow the 80–20 rule, which is to say that 20% of the information provides 80% of the value. In many cases, any extra information collected will merely reinforce and confirm what was learned from the most useful 20%. This is probably the case in Ronald's investigation of fire extinguishers.

This does not usually mean that the first 20% of the information you obtain is the most valuable. The valuable bits may be mixed up with all the rest. So how do you decide which information is worth focusing on?

Activity 8   4 mins

We can pin down what we mean by 'quality information' by considering what others expect when you provide them with information.

Suppose you have to report on a problem that has arisen in your department. Jot down six words that describe what the information you provide should be like.

_____

_____

_____

Managers use information to answer questions and, for them, quality information is that which does this quickly, simply, accurately and reliably. This means it must be relevant and thorough, but concise.

Too much information makes life more difficult, so you need a strategy for focusing in quickly on what you need to know.

Let's assume you have a pile of material on paper: notes you have made on interviews and verbal reports, written reports, data printed out from the computer system, memos, articles, background documents, statistics and so on.

There is too much to study in detail, but there might be important information lurking in any of these items.

Here is a strategy for managing paperwork.

Stage 1	Make a brief list of all the items of information (you may prefer to number the documents, as lawyers do).	This will help you **find the item** you want more quickly
Stage 2	Write down the questions you hope this information will answer.	This will help **focus your mind** during the next stages.
Stage 3	Sort the items into two roughly equal piles: 'most relevant' and 'least relevant'. Leave the 'least relevant' items aside: you won't need them unless you can't get convincing answers from the 'most relevant' pile.	You have already **halved** the amount of information you need to consider!
Stage 4	Scan/skim the 'most relevant' pile and use sticky notes or highlighters to mark those that seem most likely to give you your answers.	Save time by concentrating on **summaries**, **visual information** and **'bottom lines'** on tables.
Stage 5	Now read the important bits of the items you have highlighted in more detail.	It's advisable to **make brief notes**.

Do you now have enough information?

If not, you have either to go back to the 'least relevant' pile, or decide where else the information might come from.

Remember that the cost of getting more information may be greater than its value!

Using this five-stage approach will save you time and should help you identify the most relevant information. It will also greatly reduce the numbers of different items of information you have to manage.

3 Decision-making models

3.1 Models

A model is a representation of a real-life thing or situation.

Models allow you to experiment, and try out different scenarios to see which course of action gives the best results. They are used to provide information for decision-making when experimenting with real life is impossible, often because it depends on the future and on the actions of others.

There are a number of different sorts of model, such as an architect's miniature model of a building development. The developers will want to see something that gives them an idea of what they will be getting for the millions of pounds they are going to spend, but it would obviously be impracticable and pointlessly expensive to build a full-scale trial version, using genuine materials.

However, in everyday business, decision-making mathematical models are the most commonly used. These represent a real-life situation in terms of mathematical relationships and formulae.

A mathematical model consists of several interrelated variables. A variable is simply an item in the model that has a value.

There are different ways of categorizing variables.

- **Input variables and output variables**. Input variables are the variables in the model that interact with other variables to produce the end result, or 'output' from the model. The items of output information are output variables. The value of outputs will depend on the value of input variables, and how they inter relate.

   For instance, your ideal monthly income might be £5,000, but you might recognize that you will only earn 30% of that. The input variables are inter related by multiplying them together to produce the output variable.

   Input variable A: £5,000; Input variable B: 30%

   Inter relation formula: A × B

   Output variable: £1,500

- **Controlled and non-controlled variables**. Controlled variables are input variables whose value you can control, at least to some extent. Non-controlled variables in a model are items that you have no power to change. For instance, you can choose whether to buy supplies from an expensive supplier or a cheaper one, but you cannot control the rate of VAT.

Activity 9

Your ideal monthly income is £3,000 but you know that you will only earn 70% of that – because you are on a fixed salary!

Identify or calculate the variables in this scenario.

Input variable(s): _____

Output variable(s): _____

Controlled variable(s): _____

Non-controlled variable(s): _____

The answers to this Activity can be found on page 128.

3.2 Examples of business models

Models can be used to help with many kinds of business decision. Here are a number of possibilities.

- **Inventory models**. These help to decide the ideal amounts for stocks of materials or finished goods held, ordering quantities and re-order levels. The EOQ model, a well-known example, follows below.

- **Resource allocation models**. These help the manager to share out scarce resources between competing activities, for example to decide how much time members of the workteam should spend on task A, how much on task B, and so on. We'll look at a simple example later in the session. More complex problems need a mathematical technique called **linear programming**, but that is a little too involved for this book. Another approach is to use project management techniques such as **Gantt charts**. We will be looking at these in Session C.

- **Budget models**. These are used to prepare budgets for an organization, such as a cash budget or a breakeven model. Usually you would do this using a spreadsheet (there's an example later in the session), and perhaps some forecasting models such as those discussed in Session B.

- **Queuing models**. These simulate arrivals at and departures from a servicing point such as a till in a shop, and show how long the queues will get, depending on how many tills you have open. This can quickly get very complex and a computer is the only way to develop such a model effectively.

■ **Business plan models.** These are models used for overall planning by senior managers. Variables would include capital investments, sources of finance, interest rates, assets, liabilities, sales, costs, growth rates, and so on.

There are also modelling techniques that can be used in combination with any of the above, or simply to help you define a problem more clearly. **Probabilities/expected values** and **decision trees** are the best examples, and you'll learn the basics of these techniques before you have finished this session.

3.3 The EOQ model

One of the best-known business decision-making models is the Economic Order Quantity (EOQ) model. You may not deal with stocks in your job, but the model is a very good example of the way mathematical models can help with decisions.

The EOQ model is used to decide what quantity of stock should be ordered so as to minimize the total costs associated with holding and ordering stock. For instance, if you order 20,000 items you will need to have somewhere to keep them, and space costs money. If you order 200 items you'll need a lot less space, but you will have to go through the process of ordering items 100 times – and that administrative time costs money.

There is a formula (a mathematical model) for calculating the EOQ.

$$EOQ = \sqrt{\frac{2C_0 D}{Ch}}$$

■ C_0 = cost of ordering stocks from a supplier;
■ D = demand during the time period;
■ Ch = cost of holding one unit of stock for one time period.

You need not worry about why the formula works. All you need to do is plug the relevant numbers into it and work out the result.

Activity 10

2 mins

Suppose that Apache Ltd purchases raw materials at a cost of £15 per unit. Apache Ltd's annual demand for the raw material is 25,000 units. The holding cost per unit is £12.80 and the cost of placing each order is £16.

Calculate the EOQ using the formula and the information provided.

You should have got the answer 250. To check that this is correct, here's a table that works out the costs for various order quantities. In this table:

■ average stock = order quantity divided by 2
■ number of orders = annual demand (25,000) divided by order quantity
■ annual holding cost = average stock times £12.80
■ annual order cost = number of orders times £16

Order quantity	100	150	200	250	300	350	400
Average stock	50	75	100	125	150	175	200
Number of orders	250	166.67	125	100	83.33	71.43	62.5
	£	£	£	£	£	£	£
Annual holding cost	640	960	1,280	1,600	1,920	2,240	2,560
Annual order cost	4,000	2,667	2,000	1,600	1,333	1,143	1,000
Total cost	4,640	3,627	3,280	3,200	3,253	3,383	3,560

You can see from the table that costs are lowest at the order quantity of 250.

To save all this trial and error, here is the quick way of getting the answer: use the EOQ model!

$$\text{EOQ} = \sqrt{(2 \times £16 \times 25{,}000)/£12.80}$$

$$= \sqrt{62{,}500}$$

$$= 250$$

3.4 Resource allocation and limiting factors

A limiting factor is something that stops you doing what you'd really like to do. Money is the most obvious one: for instance if you'd like to go on holiday to the Bahamas but only have £10 to spend, then money is your limiting factor.

Other resources like time and materials may also be limiting factors. Here's a simple example.

LF Ltd makes two products, and costs are as follows.

	Product 1	**Product 2**
	£	£
Materials	20	25
Labour (£10 per hour)	20	10
Overheads	5	5
	45	40

Product 1 is sold for £60 each; product 2 for £50 each. During March 2004 the available labour is limited to 20,000 hours. Fixed costs per month are £50,000 and there are no opening stocks.

Sales demand in March is expected to be as follows.

Product 1   8,000 units
Product 2   11,000 units

We want to decide how many of each product to make to maximize profit. To do this, we must do three things.

1   Confirm that the available labour hours are indeed a limiting factor.

	Product 1	**Product 2**	**Total**
Labour hours per unit	2 hours	1 hour	
Sales demand	8,000 units	11,000 units	
Labour hours needed	16,000 hours	11,000 hours	27,000 hrs
Labour hours available			20,000 hrs
Shortfall			7,000 hrs

Labour is a limiting factor: there is a shortfall of 7,000 hours.

2 Identify the gross profit earned by each product per unit of the scarce resource, that is, per labour hour.

	Product 1 £	Product 2 £
Sales price	60	50
Variable cost	45	40
Unit gross profit	15	10
Labour hours per unit	2 hrs	1 hr
Gross profit per labour hour (i.e. per unit of limiting factor)	£7.50	£10

Although product 1 has a higher gross profit per unit than product 2, two product 2 units can be made in the time it takes to make one product 1. Because labour is in limited supply it is more profitable to make product 2 than product 1.

3 Work out the production budget. We will make enough product 2 to meet the full sales demand. The remaining labour hours available will then be used to make product 1.

Product	Demand	Hours required	Hours available	Priority for manufacture
Product 2	11,000	11,000	11,000	1st
Product 1	8,000	16,000	9,000 (balance)	2nd
		27,000	20,000	

Product	Units	Hours needed	Gross profit £	Total
Product 2	11,000	11,000	10	110,000
Product 1 (balance)	4,500	9,000	15	67,500
		20,000		177,500
Less fixed costs				50,000
Profit				127,500

Just to confirm that it is not more profitable to begin by making as many units as possible of the product with the bigger unit gross profit, suppose you make 8,000 units of product 1 (£15 per unit), using up 16,000 hours and 4,000 units of product 2 (£10 per unit) in the remaining 4,000 hours. Profit would be (£8,000 × £15) + (£4,000 × £10) − fixed costs = £160,000 − £50,000. Profit would be only £110,000.

Although it may seem tempting, unit gross profit is not the best way to decide priorities. As soon as you realize it takes two hours to earn £15 from a product 1 but only one hour to earn £10 from a product 2 it is obvious that product 2 makes better use of the limited resource.

Activity 11 · 8 mins

LF Ltd makes two products, and costs are as follows.

	Product 1	Product 2
	£	£
Materials	20	25
Labour (£10 per hour)	20	10
Overheads	4	5
	44	40

Product 1 is sold for £60 each; product 2 for £50 each. Sales demand in April is expected to be 8,000 units of product 1 and 11,000 units of product 2. During April 2004 the available labour is limited to 35,000 hours. Materials cost £5 per unit, and only 70,000 units can be purchased due to a world shortage.

How many of each product should LF Ltd make to maximize profit?

Use a separate sheet for your answer.

The answer to this Activity can be found on page 128.

3.5 Simple spreadsheet models or 'what if' analysis

Because they generally involve numbers and formulae and logic, many business models are ideally suited for computerization. Complex models will need a specialized computer package, but the familiar spreadsheet can often be used for day-to-day problems.

Once a model has been constructed and saved, the consequences of changes in any of the variables can be tested by asking 'what if' questions (this is also known as 'sensitivity analysis').

For example, a spreadsheet may be used to develop a cash flow model, such as the one below.

	A	B	C	D	E
1			Month 1	Month 2	Month 3
2	Sales	120%	5,000	6,000	7,000
3	Cost of sales	65%	-3,250	-3,900	-4,680
4	Gross profit				
5					
6	**Receipts**				
7	Current month	60%	3,000	3,600	4,320
8	1 month in arrears	40%		2,000	2,400
9	2 months in arrears	0%			0
10			3,000	5,600	6,720
11	**Payments**		-3,250	-3,900	-4,680
12			-250	1,700	2,040
13	Bank balance b/fwd		0	-250	1,450
14	Bank balance c/fwd		-250	1,450	3,490

Here are some typical 'what if' questions.

1   What if the cost of sales is 68% of sales revenue, not 65%?

2   What if payment from debtors is received as follows:

month of sale	40%
one month in arrears	50%
two months in arrears	10%

instead of 60% in the month of sale and 40% one month in arrears?

3   What if sales growth is only 15% per month instead of 20% per month?

With a spreadsheet model, the answers to questions like these can be found simply and quickly, simply by changing the variables shown as percentages.

The different scenarios give managers a better understanding of what the cash flow position in the future might be, and what they need to do to make sure the cash position remains reasonable. For example, if the company has not agreed an overdraft facility it is going to get into trouble in its very first month! Or it might be found that the cost of sales must remain less than 67% of sales value, or that sales growth of at least 10% per month is essential to achieve a satisfactory cash position.

Activity 12

10 mins

Create a spreadsheet exactly as shown above using formulae wherever appropriate. The only cells that should contain a number are the cells in column B (the variables), cell C2 (5,000) and cell C13 (0). To help you here are the formulae for Month 2.

D
Month 2
=C2*$B$2
=-D2*0.65
=SUM(D2:D3)
=D2*$B$7
=C2*$B$8
=SUM(D7:D9)
=D3
=SUM(D10:D11)
=C14
=SUM(D12:D13)

Once you have done this, save your spreadsheet. Then change the variables and answer the 'what if' questions posed above (what if sales growth is only 15% per month instead of 20% per month). Your answers should state the bank balance at the end of Month 3.

The answers to this Activity can be found on page 130.

3.6 Expected values

Expected values (or EVs) are based on probabilities (or 'expectations') and they can be very useful in decision-making, especially for decision trees, which we will tackle next.

Expected values work on the idea that if the probability of something happening is p, and the expected number of times that it will occur is n then the expected value (EV) is $n \times p$.

For instance, suppose two in every hundred products you sell are returned by customers because of a fault. Or to put it another way, it seems that the probability that a component in the product will be faulty is 0.02 (2/100).

So how many returns would we expect to get if we sold 5,000 products?

$$EV = 5,000 \times 0.02$$
$$= 100 \text{ returns to be expected.}$$

Activity 13

2 mins

The daily sales of a product may be as follows.

Units	Probability
100	0.25
150	0.30
200	0.40
300	0.05
	1.00

What are the expected daily sales?

The EV of daily sales is calculated by multiplying each possible outcome (volume of daily sales) by the probability that this outcome will occur, and then adding the results together.

Units	Probability	Expected value
100	0.25	25
150	0.30	45
200	0.40	80
300	0.05	15
	1.00	165

In the long run, the expected value should be approximately 165 units, if the event occurs many times over. In the example above, we do not expect sales on any one day to be 165 units, but in the long run, over a large number of days, and assuming we have the probabilities correct, average sales should equal 165 units a day.

3.7 Decision-making and expected values

Suppose you have to choose between some options and you are looking for the one that gives the best profit for your organization. You might think you'd simply choose the one with the highest expected value, but there are some drawbacks if you do that.

Activity 14 · 5 mins

Suppose there are two projects with the following possible profits.

Project A		Project B	
Probability	Profit/(loss) £	Probability	Profit/(loss) £
0.75	12,000	0.1	−4,800
0.25	14,400	0.2	12,000
		0.5	16,800
		0.2	19,200

Which project should be chosen?

The EV for each project is as follows.

	Project A			Project B	
Probability	Profit/(loss) £	EV £	Probability	Profit/(loss) £	EV £
0.75	12,000	9,000	0.1	−4,800	−480
0.25	14,400	3,600	0.2	12,000	2,400
			0.5	16,800	8,400
			0.2	19,200	3,840
		12,600			14,160

Project B has a higher EV. This means that, on the balance of probabilities, it could offer a better profit than A, and so is arguably a better choice.

On the other hand, if you look at the table, the minimum return from project A would be £12,000 whereas with B there is a 0.1 chance of a loss of £4,800. So project A might be a safer choice.

3.8 Decision trees

Complex problems need a clear logical approach to make sure that all possible choices and outcomes are taken into account.

Decision trees are a useful way of working through and visualizing such problems.

Decision trees are drawn from left to right, and so a decision tree will start like this.

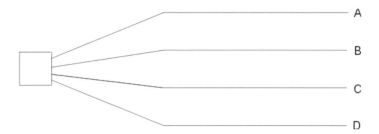

The **square** is the **decision point**, and the 'branches' A, B, C and D are four different choices. For example, your choices might be (A) to use cash to buy new computer equipment; (B) get a loan to buy it; (C) hire the equipment; or (D) continue to use existing equipment.

If a choice can have only one outcome, the branch of the decision tree for that alternative is complete. Usually, though, the choice will have several possible outcomes. We show this on a decision tree by putting in an **outcome point (a circle)** with each possible choice shown as a subsidiary branch.

The probability of each outcome occurring is written on the relevant branch.

In the example above, there are two options facing the decision-maker, A and B. If A is chosen there is only one possible outcome, but if B is chosen, there are two possible outcomes, high profits (0.7 probability) or low profits (0.3 probability).

Activity 15

In the example above, suppose you are certain that option A will give a profit of £25,000, but you are not sure whether option B will give a profit of £30,000 or £10,000. Which is the best option to choose?

_____

_____

_____

_____

The answer is option A, because option B gives an EV of (£30,000 × 0.7) + (10,000 × 0.3) = £24,000.

In this simple case we didn't really need to draw a diagram, but when there are lots of choices and options decision trees can be very helpful.

For example, sometimes, a decision taken now will mean that other decisions have to be made in the future. Say you have to choose between option A and option B, and depending on the outcome of that decision, you will later have to make a choice between C and D or else a choice between E and F.

If this is the problem you can draw a decision tree like this.

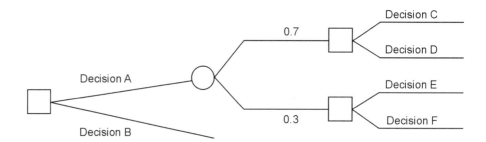

The diagram helps you to visualize and understand this problem much more clearly than the words.

That's enough theory: let's look at a full scale example.

Activity 16

15 mins

Arbor Ltd is considering developing a new product. The company can either test market the product or abandon it.

If the company test markets it, the cost will be £32,000. The market response could be either favourable or unfavourable with probabilities of 0.45 and 0.55.

If the market response is favourable the company could market the product full scale, or they could still abandon the product.

If it markets the new product full scale, the outcome might be low, medium or high demand. The net gains (or losses) would be £64,000, £78,000 or £320,000 respectively and these outcomes have probabilities of 0.21, 0.55 and 0.24 respectively.

If the result of the test marketing is unfavourable but the company goes ahead and markets the product anyway, estimated losses would be £192,000.

If, at any point, the company abandons the product, there would be a net gain of £16,000 from the sale of scrap.

Without looking at our answer see if you can draw a decision tree for the problem faced by Arbor Ltd. Include figures for cost, loss or profit on the appropriate branches of the tree. You might need to try several times, so use a separate sheet of paper for your answer.

The starting point for the tree is to establish what decision has to be made now. The options are:

■ to abandon;
■ to test market.

The outcome of the abandon option is known for certain: the sale of scrap with a net gain of £16,000.

There are two possible outcomes of the option to test market: favourable response or unfavourable response.

Depending on the outcome of the test marketing, another decision will then be made, to abandon the product or to go ahead.

This is the decision tree.

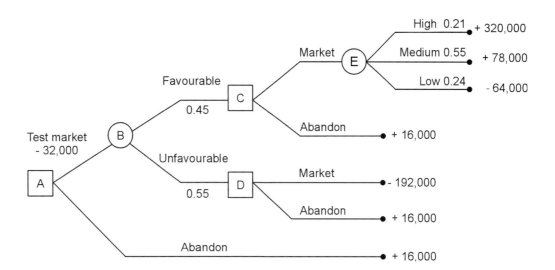

Now we have a nice tree-like diagram, and it helps us to understand the logic of the problem much more clearly. But we still haven't made a decision!

We need to evaluate the tree using expected values. The basic rules are as follows.

We start on the right-hand side of the tree, which represents the future, and work back towards the left-hand side, the decision we have to make now. (This is called the rollback technique.) At each outcome point we calculate the EV.

At **outcome point E** (the right-hand-most point) the EV is as follows.

Sales	£		£
High	320,000	0.24	76,800
Medium	78,000	0.55	42,900
Low	−64,000	0.21	−13,440
			106,260

This is the EV of the decision to market the product if the test shows favourable response. You may like to write the EV on the decision tree itself, at the appropriate outcome point (point E).

At **decision point C**, the choice is as follows.

- Full-scale marketing EV (the EV at point E) = + £106,260.
- Abandon = + £16,000.

Obviously the choice would be to market the product, and so the EV at decision point C is **+ £106,260**.

At **decision point D**, an unfavourable market reaction, the choice is as follows.

- Market anyway: loss = − £192,000.
- Abandon = + £16,000.

Obviously, the choice would be to abandon, and so the EV at decision point D is **+ £16,000**.

The later decisions have therefore been made. If the original decision is to test market, the company will market the product if the test shows favourable customer response, and will abandon the product if the test results are unfavourable.

Now we need to calculate the EV at **outcome point B**.

	£		EV £
Point C	106,260	0.45	47,817
Point D	16,000	0.55	8,800
			56,617

Finally we compare the options at **decision point A**, which are as follows.

■ Test: EV = EV at B minus test marketing cost = £56,617 – 32,000 = +£24,617
■ Abandon = +£16,000

The choice at decision point A would be to test market the product because it has a higher EV of profit. But there is a lot less in it than you may have thought.

Activity 17

4 mins

In the case of Arbor Ltd (Activity 16) what would the decision have been if the highest probable gains had been £140,000 and the probability of a favourable report had been 0.75?

The answers to this Activity can be found on page 130.

As you've probably realized, evaluating decisions by using decision trees has some limitations.

■ The outcome with the highest EV may be the riskiest course of action.
■ Managers may not be willing to take risks if they may result in losses.
■ The probabilities are guesses, and they may well be wrong.

Self-assessment 1

1 Say which of these **two** statements is correct and which is incorrect; give reasons for your answer.

    a Top management should know every detail of what is going on in their organization.

    _____

    _____

    _____

    b Workteams don't necessarily need to know every detail about what is going on in the wider organization, but it may be a good idea to keep them well-informed.

    _____

    _____

    _____

2 What are the six stages of the decision-making process?

    Stage 1 _____

    Stage 2 _____

    Stage 3 _____

    Stage 4 _____

    Stage 5 _____

    Stage 6 _____

3 Complete this statement about the pros and cons of acquiring more information by inserting the letter (A, B etc.) of the appropriate phrase.

Phrases:

A creates problems in itself
B obtaining, sorting and evaluating
C to make decisions
D acquiring more information
E we don't have enough

We need information _____, but usually _____ information to make good decisions. That means _____, but too much information _____, because the costs of _____ it can be greater than its value.

4 When a resource is in short supply there is a three step method for deciding the best production strategy. What are the three steps?

Step 1: _____

Step 2: _____

Step 3: _____

5 A business decision model usually represents a real-life situation in terms of _____. The model will consist of _____. A model allows you to try out _____ to see _____.

Fill in the missing words.

6 Out of 260 working days last year, your workteam was one person short through sickness on 23 days. If your workteam has 10 members including yourself and everyone works seven hours a day, how many hours' work would you expect to get out of your workteam in a typical 22 working day month?

_____

7 Fill in the missing words or phrases below using the appropriate term from the list. You may need to use some terms more than once while you may not use others at all. The terms are:

an outcome point; square; left; circle; a decision point; right

When drawing a decision tree a _____ is used as the symbol for _____, and a _____ is used as the symbol for a decision point. The branches from _____ have probabilities assigned to them. A decision tree is evaluated from _____ to _____.

Answers to these questions can be found on page 124.

4 Summary

■ Organizations function because people provide each other with information and act on it. The type of information used by senior managers is different from the type used by operational managers.

■ The decision-making process typically has six stages:

1 problem recognition;
2 problem definition and structuring;
3 identifying alternative courses of action;
4 making and communicating the decision;
5 implementing the decision;
6 reviewing the effects of the decision.

■ Managers rarely have all the information they might like, but it is not always worthwhile to obtain extra information. The costs should be weighed up against the benefits.

■ Models in business are usually mathematical models consisting of variables and mathematical formulae.

■ Examples of business models include inventory models, resource allocation models, budget models, queuing models and business plan models.

■ Probabilities, expected values and decision trees may be used to help define and evaluate complex problems.

Session B
Analysing information

1 Introduction

Most of this session (and some of the next) is about how you can analyse numerical information – how to analyse it in ways that will probably be very familiar such as totals and percentages and how you can use basic statistics to gain a better understanding of it.

You may have bad memories of statistics if you've ever done any before, but don't worry. Mostly we'll be suggesting that you use a spreadsheet to do the painful calculations – all you have to do is enter a few figures and understand what the results mean.

We'll also look at some of the **tools** available in **spreadsheets** and spreadsheet **databases** that help you to sort, filter and analyse large amounts of data at the touch of a button. Spreadsheets also have a **charting** tool that can produce a wide variety of graphs and diagrams that help with data analysis, but we'll save that for **Session C** on data presentation.

Finally, we'll spend a short while thinking about how non-numerical data – generally words – can be analysed by imposing various structures on it and using cross-references and indexes.

1.1 Data and information

Facts and figures are called **data**.

Information is processed data.

Items of data do not usually convey any meaning on their own. Here is an example of data.

213   242   299   359   592

Activity 18   2 mins

What do these numbers and letters tell you?

_____

_____

_____

The best that most people could say is that there are five numbers rising by different amounts and ranging from 213 to 592. They could mean almost anything: the number of passengers on different trains; the weekly wages of five different employees. They could be dates (21 March, 24 February, February 1999, and so on).

Even if you happened to know what these numbers are they don't tell you anything on their own without further analysis.

Information is data that has been **analysed or processed** in some way so as to become **meaningful**, like this.

Country name	International dialling code
Algeria	213
Congo	242
Greenland	299
Bulgaria	359
Guyana	592

This data has simply been organized into a table with column headings and labels, but now you know exactly what it means.

Activity 19

I min

How could the data be even better organized?

The answer to this Activity can be found on page 131.

2 Analysing numerical data

EXTENSION I
Managing Information and Statistics by Roland Bee and Frances Bee is helpful for those needing to know more about this area of management.

Businesses generate extensive amounts of numerical data, for example number of products sold, number of hours worked. Most of it also has a **price,** so that it can be expressed in terms of **money,** and a **date**, so that we know that we are talking about events this year (or month or week), not some other period.

In most organizations this information is collected by the accounting system, and modern accounting software has highly sophisticated reporting capabilities. Analysing numerical data on a day-to-day basis may often simply be a case of knowing which buttons to press.

In this section, we are concerned with the less routine tasks of management. One example is analysing a collection of data that is not formally recorded by the accounting system, for example how long it takes to do a set of tasks in a new way. You may need to analyse it so that you can make some **decision**.

Preparing next year's budget is a typical example: you have plenty of data about this year to work with, but you need to know how typical it is, whether the figures can be improved, how you can identify trends that will help you forecast the future. For this you need to know a little about statistics.

Statistics is a word that frightens many people, and at an advanced level it can get very difficult. Most business statistics, however, involve simple techniques such as adding, subtracting multiplying and dividing. You did a fair bit of that in Session A. And as you probably know, a spreadsheet can take almost all the effort out of handling numbers.

Activity 20

20 mins

Create a new folder on your computer with a name such as 'Information_ in_Management_Session_B'. Each time you create a new spreadsheet for an Activity in this session save the file with a name such as 'Activity_20'.

To start off your folder create a spreadsheet that demonstrates that you have the following basic skills. If necessary use the Help system in your spreadsheet to find out how to do them. Print out any help pages you use.

- Enter numbers and format them, for instance make them display as 1,234 (comma format) or 5.67 (to two decimal places) or as a percentage (25% instead of 0.25).
- Enter dates such as 24/03/2004.
- Enter text.
- Select cells, copy and paste their contents and drag them to other parts of the spreadsheet.
- Sum a column of numbers.
- Automatically fill in data based on adjacent cells.
- Multiply a column of numbers by the same figure using absolute cell references (for instance, A1*$C$1, A2*$C$1).

Note down the name and location of your 'basic skills' spreadsheet file here.

2.1 Ratios, indexes and percentages

It is often useful to measure one set of data against another to create a ratio or index.

For example, a business that occupies 128,000m^2 of floor space and turns over £3,968,000 has a floor space to turnover ratio of 128:3,968. Last year the ratio was 125:3,375, while the average for businesses of this type was 1:36.

We can simplify these rather clumsy expressions by dividing the first number into the second (for instance 3,968/128 = 31). This gives us:

- this year's ratio (1:31);
- last year's ratio (1:27);
- the average for businesses of this type (1:36).

By reducing all the ratios to the same numerical base (i.e. 1), we make them easy to compare. This information shows us that the business is using its floor space more efficiently than last year, but not as efficiently as its competitors.

One of the best-known ratios is **profitability**, which is profit:capital employed (it is also known as return on capital employed, or ROCE).

Activity 21

4 mins

The table below shows the capital employed and annual profit of six different companies. Work out the profitability ratio and profit percentage and enter the figures in the blank columns. Calculate ratios to the nearest whole number and percentages to one decimal point. We have done the first calculation for you.

1   Profitability ratio = 995,400 / 15.80 = 1:63,000
(This gives a ratio of profit per £ million capital employed.)

2   Profit percentage = (995,400 / 15,800,000) × 100% = 6.3%
(This gives rate of profit per £100 capital employed.)

Company	Capital employed (£m)	2004 profit (£)	Capital:profit ratio	Profit %
A	15.80	995,400	1:63,000	6.3
B	5.90	324,500	1:	
C	44.20	5,348,200	1:	
D	21.40	2,461,000	1:	
E	0.85	79,000	1:	
F	87.00	13,746,000	1:	

Most profitable: _____

Least profitable: _____

The answer to this Activity can be found on page 131.

You will probably realize, having done this Activity, that percentages are often easier to understand than ratios, though the calculation is much the same.

Ratios and percentages are both ways of presenting relationships so as to make it easier to compare figures. Here is another example.

	2003				2004	
	Qtr 1	**Qtr 2**	**Qtr 3**	**Qtr 4**	**Qtr 1**	**Qtr 2**
Revenue (£000s)	1,630	1,752	1,871	2,558	1,595	1,804
Headcount	49	47	44	57	40	40

Look across the table rows and see how both sets of figures are going up and down. We can probably assume that this is a seasonal business which performs strongly in the period up to Christmas and experiences a sharp fall afterwards. Extra staff members are taken on for the Christmas quarter.

On their own, these figures tell us nothing about the efficiency of this business. However, if we create a ratio of **revenue per headcount** (in other words divide revenue by headcount), the picture becomes much clearer.

Ratio of revenue to headcount

	2003				2004	
	Qtr 1	**Qtr 2**	**Qtr 3**	**Qtr 4**	**Qtr 1**	**Qtr 2**
	£000	£000	£000	£000	£000	£000
£000s per head	33.27	37.28	42.52	44.88	39.88	45.10

Later in this session we'll see how we might predict Quarter 4 sales in 2004, when we look at forecasting and moving averages.

Productivity is another good example of the value of ratios. We calculate it as a measure of output against a measure of labour. Output is usually measured in units, while labour may be measured in various ways, such as:

- payroll headcount;
- payroll cost;
- hours worked;
- cost per head.

These four ratios may produce somewhat different results, as the next Activity will show.

Activity 22

10 mins

Period	1	2	3	4	5	Average
Data						
Output (units)	217.0	221.0	229.0	214.0	233.0	
Headcount	61.0	61.0	59.0	51.0	51.0	
Cost (£'000s)	119.6	125.3	125.1	119.5	131.3	
Hours worked	2,318.0	2,379.0	2,315.0	2,116.0	2167.0	
Indexes						
Output per head	—					
Cost per unit of output						
Hours worked per unit						
Cost per head						

Work out the productivity indexes and averages, and insert them in the blank spaces in the table. Show your answers to two decimal places.

What do the indexes and averages show?

_____

_____

_____

_____

_____

The correct version of the table, and our interpretation, can be found on page 131.

Note that measuring, recording and producing indexes from this data – that is, **analysing** it – has resulted in:

■ a clear picture of how the productivity position has been changing;
■ recognition that there is a problem;
■ a clear identification of where the problem lies.

2.2 What is 'typical'?

Managers can learn a lot from figures using the simplest of techniques: counting, adding, dividing, and calculating percentages and indexes.

Usually this involves putting data into some kind of table and working out totals and averages. (We'll talk in general about how to lay out tables in Session C: you have already seen lots of examples in this session and the last.)

Let's take, as a very basic example, interviews conducted by three staff at a government office. The staff members work a five-day, 37.5 hour week.

Activity 23

4 mins

We start by counting how many interviews each person carried out each day.

Work out the totals and enter them in the blank column of the table below. (The average (or 'mean') is the total divided by the number of working days. Do the average to one decimal place.)

These calculations can easily be done by hand using a calculator, but if you have access to a spreadsheet, this is a better option. For example, if you start entering data at cell A1 you could use the formulae =SUM(B2:F2) and =AVERAGE(B2:F2).

Staff	Interviews conducted per day					Total	Average
	Monday	Tuesday	Wednesday	Thursday	Friday		
Dela	45	43	44	21	46		
Corinne	54	50	51	55	53		
David	38	41	40	44	39		

The answer to this Activity can be found on page 132.

Next we add some extra data for comparison purposes, showing target performance – the number of interviews each person is expected to carry out.

We can now do some more complex and informative calculations:

■ the percentage of target performance achieved (actual performance divided by target performance × 100%);
■ the average performance.

Activity 24

6 mins

Work out these percentages and averages and enter them in this table to show performance against target. Work to one decimal place. Use a spreadsheet and SUM and AVERAGE formulae if possible, and don't forget to save your spreadsheet, for your portfolio evidence, if you do.

Staff	Interviews conducted per day						
	Monday	Tuesday	Wednesday	Thursday	Friday	Total	Average
Dela							
Actual	45.0	43.0	44.0	21.0	46.0		
Target	52.5	52.5	52.5	52.5	52.5		
% of target						n/a	
Corinne							
Actual	54.0	50.0	51.0	55.0	53.0		
Target	52.5	52.5	52.5	52.5	52.5		
% of target						n/a	
David							
Actual	38.0	41.0	40.0	44.0	39.0		
Target	38.0	38.0	38.0	38.0	38.0		
% of target						n/a	

The answer to this Activity can be found on page 132.

By processing the data in these quite simple ways, we can obtain some useful information from them.

- How each person is performing against target.
- How each person is performing against the departmental average.

The new figures also reveal some unexplained oddities.

Activity 25

2 mins

Note down two things that strike you as odd about the final figures.

_____

_____

There are two obvious points.

- On Thursday, Dela's performance fell sharply to 21 interviews.
- David's target figures are lower than those for the other two staff.

Managers are always looking for deviations from what is expected, so these two oddities need to be explained. An investigation may discover, for instance, that Dela was sick for an afternoon, and that David is a trainee who has been set lower targets initially. Or perhaps Dela spent an afternoon sitting with David, helping with training.

Whatever the case it would be a good idea to include explanations with the table and analysis, if you are reporting to your own manager about your team's performance.

2.3 Measures of central tendency

You hear about averages all the time – average income, average lifespan, average number of goals per game or runs per innings, and so on.

Averages like this can be useful because they can often answer the question 'what is typical?'.

The most common type of average is more properly called the **arithmetic mean**, and it is very easy to calculate: you simply find the total of the numbers, then divide by the number of values. If you have three values, 1, 2 and 3, the total is 6 and so the arithmetic mean is 6 divided by 3, which equals 2: (1 + 2 + 3) / 3 = 2.

However, an average like this can be 'mean' in the sense that it doesn't tell you all you need to know: it can be misleading. The performance figures we just looked at for Dela are a case in point. It is important for her manager to know her typical performance against target, but averaging her across five days does not give an accurate idea of what is typical.

Because Dela only worked for half the day on Thursday, her average performance over five days comes out as 75.8%. If we'd omitted Thursday, her average would be 84.8%, and this is a truer reflection of her performance.

The mean can easily be distorted by the inclusion of one or more untypical figures, so it sometimes helps to use a different measure of centrality.

Two alternatives to the mean are the **median** and the **mode**.

- The **median** is the **middle value** in a series.
- The **mode** is the value which appears **most often** in a series.

Activity 26 · 2 mins

179   199   202   229   249   263   263   263   277

In the nine-value series above, determine the average (arithmetic mean), the median and the mode.

_____

_____

_____

What formulae would you use to determine the arithmetic mean (average), the median, and the mode if these figures were entered in cells A1 to A9 of a spreadsheet? (This question is much easier than you might think!)

_____

_____

_____

The answers to this Activity can be found on page 133.

There is sometimes a case for saying that either the median or the mode provides a more meaningful answer to the question 'what is typical?' than the mean does.

2.4 Grouped data

Suppose you measure the daily demand for a product you are selling over 20 days and then want to analyse the results to find typical daily demand. For instance, in the following results there were two days when daily demand was 14.

Daily demand	Frequency
14	2
22	2
24	1
27	1
30	3
31	6
32	2
33	1
39	1
50	1

How can you calculate the average?

One way, of course, is not to group the data like this in the first place. You could simply list out a value for each of the 20 days and divide the sum by 20.

A quicker way, however – and sometimes the only way, depending on the data – is to multiply daily demand by frequency and then divide by 20.

Daily demand (x)	Frequency (f)	Daily demand times frequency (fx)
14	2	28
22	2	44
24	1	24
27	1	27
30	3	90
31	6	186
32	2	64
33	1	33
39	1	39
50	1	50
	20	585

The average is 585/20 = 29.25.

This technique becomes especially useful if you are asked to work out an average from data that is collected in **class** intervals. For instance, using the previous example data might have been shown as follows.

Daily demand	Frequency
I to 10	0
II to 20	2
21 to 30	7
31 to 40	10
41 to 50	1
	20

This makes it more difficult to find the average because a certain amount of detail has been lost. To calculate the average when we have grouped data like this we need to decide which value best represents all of the values in a particular class interval.

It is a convention in statistics to take the mid-point of each class interval, on the assumption that the frequencies occur pretty evenly.

Daily demand	Mid point x	Frequency f	fx
I to 10	5	0	0
II to 20	15	2	30
21 to 30	25	7	175
31 to 40	35	10	350
41 to 50	45	1	45
		20	600

Arithmetic mean = 600/20 = 30.

Because our assumption that frequencies occur evenly within each class interval was not quite correct, this answer is not exactly right, but it is pretty close to the actual average of 29.25 (and we probably can't sell 0.25 of a product anyway).

In fact, although we won't demonstrate it, as the frequencies get larger (for instance, if you measured a year's worth of daily sales), the size of this error would steadily get smaller.

Activity 27

5 mins

In a particular week, the wages earned by 69 employees were as follows.

Wages	Number of employees
Up to £150	4
£151 to £160	10
£161 to £170	12
£171 to £180	13
£181 to £190	16
£191 to £200	8
£201 or more	6
	69

Calculate the arithmetic mean wage of these employees.

We don't know the mid point of the range 'under £150' but since all other class intervals are £10 we assume it is £145. Likewise we assume the mid-point of the range '£201 or more' is £205.

Mid-point £	Frequency	Mid-point × Frequency
145	4	580
155	10	1,550
165	12	1,980
175	13	2,275
185	16	2,960
195	8	1,560
205	6	1,230
	69	12,135

The arithmetic mean is 12,135/69 = £175.87.

2.5 The range

Unfortunately there are situations where focusing on one typical or central number, such as the mean, median or mode, still doesn't really help us understand what is going on.

In such a case we need to look at the **spread** of the data.

Measures of spread (or dispersion) give you some idea of how widely the data you have is spread about its average.

The **range**, for instance, is simply the difference between the highest value and the lowest value.

Activity 28

20 mins

Calculate the mean and the range of each of the following sets of data. (The range can be calculated on a spreadsheet using a formula such as =MAX(A1:A8)–MIN(A1:A8).)

1   4, 8, 7, 3, 5, 16, 24, 5

2   10, 7, 9, 11, 11, 8, 9, 7

What do your calculations show about the spread of the data?

_____

_____

_____

_____

1   The first set of eight figures add up to 72, so they have a mean of 9. The range is 24 – 3 = 21.

2   The second set of eight figures add up to 72, so they also have a mean of 9. However, the range is 11 – 7 = 4.

The first set of data is more widely dispersed than the second set. The lower the range, the less widely spread the data is.

2.6 Percentiles

Percentiles are another way of identifying the range within which most of the values in a collection of data occur. A percentile is a number that a certain percentage of the values are less than or equal to.

58	63	71	74	77	79	82	83	86	91	93
0%	10%	20%	30%	40%	50%	60%	70%	80%	90%	100%

For instance, take the value 71 in the series of numbers above. Out of the remaining ten numbers two are lower, so 71 is called the 20th percentile.

Important percentiles are the **median** (50%), the **lower quartile** (25%) and the **upper quartile** (75%).

Quartiles are a commonly-used way of identifying the range within which the values in a set of data occur. Quartiles often are used in sales and market research, and in education.

Older textbooks usually explain how you can estimate quartiles by counting up the number of values or by drawing a graph (an 'ogive'), but this is not very helpful in practice, where you are likely to have a large amount of data to analyse.

Fortunately, these days, you don't have to approximate: you can get an accurate figure for any percentile you like simply by using a spreadsheet.

Activity 29 · 15 mins

Suppose you have a set of values in cells B2 to B2357 of a spreadsheet. How would you calculate the lower quartile, the median and the upper quartile using spreadsheet facilities?

(Hint: as usual, this is not as hard as you might think!)

_____

_____

_____

You can do this in Microsoft Excel using formulae.

=QUARTILE(B2:B2357,1) will give you the lower quartile.
=QUARTILE(B2:B2357,2) will give you the median.
=QUARTILE(B2:B2357,3) will give you the upper quartile.

For the median you can also use =MEDIAN(B2:B2357,2).

Note that this will not work in all spreadsheet packages and you will need to consult your package's 'Help' facility if you are using another package.

Activity 30

15 mins

Here is a set of sales results for a week in December and a week in June for 15 sales staff. The product is a seasonal one, which sells much better in the summer. Identify the lower and upper quartiles and the median for each sitting and suggest how these figures might be used.

December 2003	June 2004
4	39
14	40
16	48
18	54
20	55
22	67
23	69
25	73
26	78
29	78
31	78
33	80
39	81
42	94
47	97

Identify the lower and upper quartiles and the median for each period and suggest how these figures might be used.

_____

_____

_____

_____

_____

Using a spreadsheet we find the following values.

	December 2003	**June 2004**
Lower quartile	19	54.5
Median	25	73
Upper quartile	32	79

This information could prove useful in planning sales targets.

In December 2004 you might set the target at the median figure of 25 units.

In June 2005, however, anyone who was selling at a rate of about 25 units in December might be expected to sell around 73 units.

Any of the sales staff who sold fewer than 55 in June would be falling seriously below target, while anyone who achieved sales of more than 79 units might be eligible for a high sales for the month award. Similar figures could be calculated for December rates of sales.

2.7 The inter-quartile range

The lower and upper quartiles can be used to calculate a measure of dispersion called the inter-quartile range. The inter-quartile range is the difference between the values of the upper and lower quartiles and hence shows the range of values of the **middle half** of the set of data. The smaller the inter-quartile range, the less dispersed the data. Because values at the ends are not taken into account, the inter-quartile range is not affected by extreme values.

For example, if the lower and upper quartiles of a set of numbers were 6 and 11, the inter-quartile range would be 11 − 6 = 5. This shows that the range of values of the middle half of the population is 5 units.

2.8 The standard deviation

EXTENSION 2
For more help with statistics, Lloyd Jaisingh's *Statistics for the Utterly Confused* is a good guide.

Because it only uses the middle 50% of the data, the inter-quartile range can be a useful measure of spread if there are extreme values.

However, it may often seem unreasonable to exclude 50% of the data.

The standard deviation (SD) is a measure of the amount by which the values in a set of numbers differ from the arithmetic mean. It is calculated using **all** of the data, not just half of it. You can calculate the SD manually or using a scientific calculator, but the easiest way is to use a spreadsheet.

Activity 31

Most of the following numbers are in the range 50 to 75, but there are some extreme values at either end.

Enter the numbers into cells A1 to A10 of a spreadsheet and find the standard deviation using the formula =STDEVP(A1:A10). Work to two decimal places.

5   20   52   60   62   64   72   72   82   151

You should get the answer **36.88** (rounded).

Although this might not look like a very meaningful number the standard deviation is actually an incredibly useful statistic because it can be proved that:

■ **68%** of the values in a set of numbers will fall within **one standard deviation** of the arithmetic mean;
■ **95%** of the values in a set of numbers will fall within **two standard deviations** of the mean.

Once you know this, the SD can be used in a wide variety of business situations, simply by collecting a relatively small sample of data: for example, in quality control, to predict future performance and prepare budgets. (We won't go into the theory, which is quite complex.)

One of the other workbooks in this series, *Achieving Quality*, explains the theory behind the standard deviation, and some of its practical uses, in more detail.

In this case the arithmetic mean is **64**. The only value that is beyond 2 standard deviations is the very extreme value 151.

−2SD	−1 SD	Mean	+1 SD	+2SD
−9.76	27.12	64	100.88	137.76

2.9 Forecasting and moving averages

Finally, in this 'statistics' part of the session, we'll take a look at another use of averages to help manage a business – averages to help with anticipating the future.

One of the most important forecasts an organization has to make is the sales forecast. How can an organization estimate how much it is likely to sell?

There are several mathematical techniques for sales forecasting such as regression analysis and exponential smoothing, which are a bit too complex for this book. Here we will concentrate on **moving averages** and **time series analysis**. The idea behind calculating a moving average is to eliminate seasonal variations.

Suppose that sales of a product for the past four years have been as follows.

Year	Season	Sales (£)
2000	Spring	5,100
	Summer	2,900
	Autumn	7,600
	Winter	4,600
2001	Spring	5,300
	Summer	3,600
	Autumn	7,500
	Winter	4,300
2002	Spring	4,900
	Summer	3,900
	Autumn	7,800
	Winter	5,200
2003	Spring	5,400
	Summer	3,800
	Autumn	8,500
	Winter	4,900

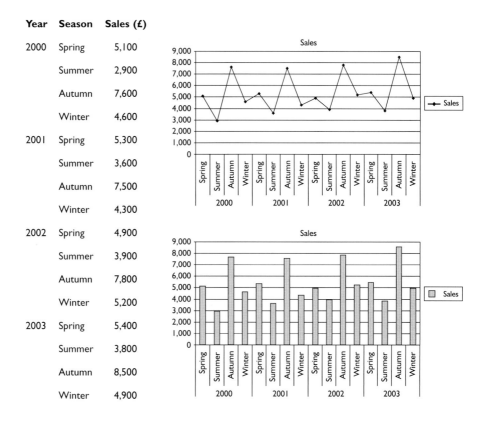

A clear pattern can be seen, especially if you look at the graph or the bar chart. But how can this organization forecast sales for 2004?

Using the moving averages technique, you begin by establishing what the seasonal cycle is. Here it is the four seasons of the year and a one year cycle. (In another situation, it might be a weekly cycle of seven days).

Next, you calculate the **moving average** of 12-monthly sales, and from this, the moving average of seasonal sales. The idea behind calculating a moving average is to eliminate seasonal variations.

Moving averages are matched against the **mid-point** of the time period to which they relate. The figures in the table are explained below it.

			Four season total	Centred average	Seasonal average (Trend)	Variation
2000	Spring	5,100				
	Summer	2,900				
			20,200			
	Autumn	7,600		20,300	5075.0	2525.0
			20,400			
	Winter	4,600				
			Etc.			
2001	Spring	5,300				

- **Four season total:** the first figure is the sum of the sales for Spring to Winter 2000 (5,100 + 2,900 + 7,600 + 4,600 = 20,200); the second is the sum of sales for Summer 2000 to Spring 2001 (2,900 + 7,600 + 4,600 + 5,300 = 20,400), and so on.

- **Centred average:** a new average is then obtained and lined up directly with the appropriate time period by taking a further average of each pair of total 12-monthly sales, for instance the average of the first two totals 20,200 and 20,400 is 20,300.

- **Seasonal average or trend:** this is simply the centred average divided by the number of seasons: 20,300/4 = 5,075. This shows the underlying long-term movement in the values. In this example we can now see clearly that there is an underlying upward trend in sales.

- **Variation:** this is the difference between the seasonal average and the actual sales: 7,600 − 5,075 = 2,525.

However, to make the data easy to set up on a spreadsheet, it is better to set it out as shown below.

		Four season total	Centred average	Seasonal average (Trend)	Variation
2000	Spring	5,100			
	Summer	2,900			
	Autumn	7,600		20,300	5075.0	2,525.0
	Winter	4,600	20,200	20,750	5187.5	−587.5
2001	Spring	5,300	20,400	21,050	5262.5	37.5
	Summer	3,600	21,100	20,850	5212.5	−1,612.5
	Autumn	7,500	21,000	20,500	5125.0	2,375.0
	Winter	4,300	20,700	20,450	5112.5	−812.5
2002	Spring	4,900	20,300	20,750	5187.5	−287.5
	Summer	3,900	20,600	21,350	5337.5	−1,437.5
	Autumn	7,800	20,900	22,050	5512.5	2,287.5
	Winter	5,200	21,800	22,250	5562.5	−362.5
2003	Spring	5,400	22,300	22,550	5637.5	−237.5
	Summer	3,800	22,200	22,750	5687.5	−1,887.5
	Autumn	8,500	22,900			
	Winter	4,900	22,600			

The difference between the actual sales in each period and the trend is the **seasonal variation** in actual sales from the average seasonal sales. To obtain a best estimate of the future variation in sales each season, we now take the simple average of these figures, as follows (figures in round brackets are negative numbers).

	Spring	Summer	Autumn	Winter
Variation				
2000			2,525.0	(587.5)
2001	37.5	(1,612.5)	2,375.0	(812.5)
2002	(287.5)	(1,437.5)	2,287.5	(362.5)
2003	(237.5)	(1,887.5)		
Total	(487.5)	(4,937.5)	7,187.5	(1,762.5)
Average (divide by 3)	(162.5)	(1,645.8)	2,395.8	(587.5)

This gives us our estimated seasonal variations in sales for each season, above or below the average seasonal sales.

If we now estimate the total sales for 2004 to be, say 23,000 units, our detailed sales forecast for 2004 would be as follows.

	Average per quarter Units	Seasonal variation Units	Sales forecast Units
Spring	5,750	(162.5)	5,587.5
Summer	5,750	(1,645.8)	4,104.2
Autumn	5,750	2,395.8	8,145.8
Winter	5,750	(587.5)	5,162.5
	23,000	0.0	23,000.0

Activity 32

30 mins

1 Enter the original three columns of data for sales between 2000 and 2003 on a spreadsheet in cells A2 to C17. Then enter formulae to calculate the remaining figures shown above. You will have to give some further thought to layout to do this effectively.

2 Using your spreadsheet estimate the sales pattern for 2004 on the basis that the organization expects annual sales to be around 28,000 units.

The answer to this Activity can be found on page 133.

3 Excel and data analysis

EXTENSION 3
Excel 2002 for Dummies is a very clear reference guide for this program.

In this section we are going to look at some of the features of spreadsheets that make them incredibly useful for analysing data. In particular we are discussing Microsoft Excel, by far the world's most popular spreadsheet program with more than 90% of the market.

3.1 Sorting and filtering

Suppose you have some raw materials stock data such as the following.

	A	B	C	D
1	Part number	Used in product	Supplier	Net cost per unit
2	18922	B	Stanger plc	15.44
3	21515	C	AJD Ltd	9.11
4	26686	B	Misto Bros	18.92
5	33019	A	Zeneca	19.63
6	47043	D	Wensley Ltd	23.75
7	51436	A	AJD Ltd	6.37
8	78053	D	Denver & Co	36.30
9	83779	B	Wensley Ltd	28.15
10				

This data is currently sorted in ascending numerical order of part number (column A), but it doesn't have to stay like that. For instance, if you wanted to know what parts were used in what products it would be better to re-sort the data in ascending order of column B.

To do this you simply select all the data, click on **Data . . . Sort** and change the **Sort by** column.

Activity 33

10 mins

Enter the data shown above into a spreadsheet and sort it by product. Save your spreadsheet because you will use it again in the next Activity.

You should get the following result.

	A	B	C	D
1	Part number	Used in product	Supplier	Net cost per unit
2	33019	A	Zeneca	19.63
3	51436	A	AJD Ltd	6.37
4	18922	B	Stanger plc	15.44
5	26686	B	Misto Bros	18.92
6	83779	B	Wensley Ltd	28.15
7	21515	C	AJD Ltd	9.11
8	47043	D	Wensley Ltd	23.75
9	78053	D	Denver & Co	36.30
10				

This is a very useful technique for small amounts of data and for data that you have to enter in a random fashion initially, for instance if you were creating the spreadsheet from a large pile of paper documents in no particular order.

Usually, though, you would have a lot more data than this – perhaps thousands and thousands of rows – and it may very well be inconvenient to resort to it all the time. You would probably want to leave it in part number order.

If that's the case then a better tool is the **AutoFilter** facility. To use this, all you have to do is select your data and click on **Data . . .AutoFilter**, and the following happens.

	A	B	C	D
1	Part number ▾	Used in product ▾	Supplier ▾	Net cost per unit ▾
2	18922	B	Stanger plc	15.44
3	21515	C	AJD Ltd	9.11
4	26686	B	Misto Bros	18.92
5	33019	A	Zeneca	19.63
6	47043	D	Wensley Ltd	23.75
7	51436	A	AJD Ltd	6.37
8	78053	D	Denver & Co	36.30
9	83779	B	Wensley Ltd	28.15

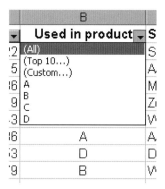

The little downward pointing arrows at the head of each column allows you to choose exactly what data is shown.

For instance, if you just want to see what parts are used in product D, you can just click on the arrow in column B and select D.

Activity 34 · 15 mins

Open the spreadsheet you created for the last Activity. Sort the data by Part number and then AutoFilter it. Using the downward arrows find out which parts are used only in product D and how much the materials for product D cost in total.

You should find that parts **47043** and **78053** are used in product D and the total cost is £60.05. (You can use the SUM button to find the total cost if you like.) Although in this case you could probably see the answer without doing any filtering, imagine if there were 20,000 different parts and 100 products and each product needed 50 or so components!

To restore the original data all you need to do is click on the arrow in column B again and select **All**.

It is also well worth learning how to do a custom filter. For instance, suppose you wanted to identify the numbers of all parts that cost more than £25. To do this click on the arrow in column D and select **Custom**. The following dialog is displayed.

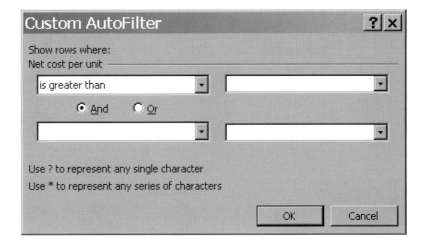

You have lots of filtering options here: show rows where the value is greater than or less than a certain amount; show rows where the values begin with a certain letter; and so on.

Activity 35 · 10 mins

Filter your spreadsheet so that it shows only parts that cost more than £25. What are the part numbers?

You should get the answer 78053 and 83779.

It is well worth spending a few more minutes experimenting with filters. For example, see if you can show only parts used in product A that cost less than £10.

3.2 Pivot Tables

Microsoft Excel has a very powerful data analysis tool called a PivotTable. There isn't space to tell you about this in great depth, but with a little basic knowledge you should be able to discover its many uses for yourself by experimentation.

PivotTables are useful when there are several different ways to analyse the data you have in front of you.

For example, the spreadsheet below shows sales data by month, by salesperson, and by type of product sold. Some of the data is numerical, some is text.

	A	B	C	D	E
1	Month	Salesperson	Blue	Green	All items
2	May	Alfred	75	125	200
3	May	Bonnie	25	75	100
4	May	Clyde	53	97	150
5	June	Alfred	100	200	300
6	June	Bonnie	50	100	150

If you wanted to know how many products Alfred sold in total you can't see this at a glance. (In this case it's not difficult to work out, but again that's because we are only showing you a small amount of data: if there were 100 salespeople, 25 products and 12 months of data it would be very hard to see at a glance!)

Creating a PivotTable is a little more complex than filtering. Once you have entered the data above in a spreadsheet select cells A1 to E6 and click on **Data . . . PivotTable** and **PivotChartReport . . . .**

An Excel Wizard then appears to take you through the steps.

■ At Step 1 make sure the options selected are **Microsoft Excel list** or **database** and **PivotTable** and click on **Next**.
■ At Step 2 the Range A1 to E6 should already be entered (because you selected those cells before you started) so just click on **Next**.
■ At Step 3 select **Existing worksheet** and click on cell G1. Then click on the **Layout** button. The following dialog will appear.

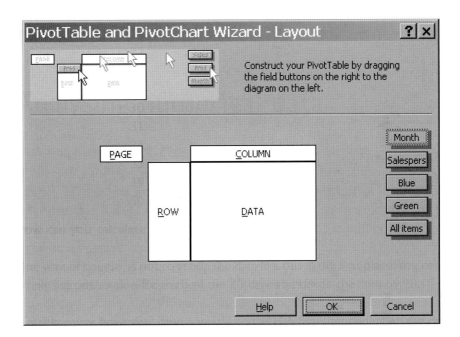

This is a bit confusing. It's very unclear what you should do next. The best way to learn is by following the simple instructions in Activity 36.

Activity 36

Before you read on, enter the data shown above in a new spreadsheet file and then follow the steps up until you get to the dialog shown above.

Let's suppose that you'd been asked to prepare an analysis of monthly sales per salesperson for each product. In other words analyse the data three ways: by month (text), by salesperson (text), and by products sold (numbers).

If you think about it like this the point of the Layout grid starts to get a bit clearer. Let's put textual data in the ROW and COLUMN areas, and numerical data in the DATA area, as shown below. We will not include the All items field button for now, but only to keep things simple.

All you have to do is drag and drop the buttons into the appropriate area of the layout grid until it looks like this.

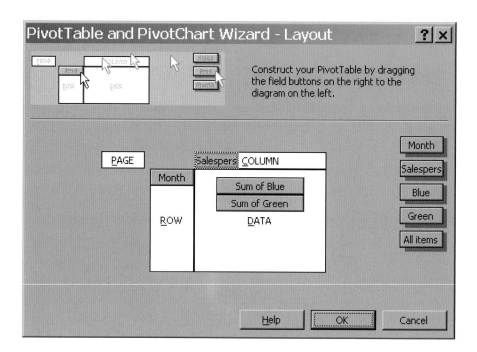

Click on **OK** on this dialog to take you back to Step 3 of the Wizard and click on **Finish**. The result is a PivotTable.

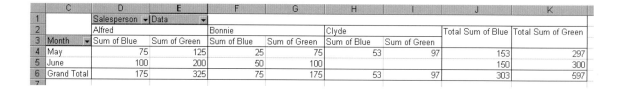

	C	D	E	F	G	H	I	J	K
1		Salesperson ▾	Data ▾						
2		Alfred		Bonnie		Clyde		Total Sum of Blue	Total Sum of Green
3	Month ▾	Sum of Blue	Sum of Green	Sum of Blue	Sum of Green	Sum of Blue	Sum of Green		
4	May	75	125	25	75	53	97	153	297
5	June	100	200	50	100			150	300
6	Grand Total	175	325	75	175	53	97	303	597
7									

The PivotTable gives us a variety of information that it is not so easy to see at a glance from the original data, for instance:

- how many Blues Alfred sold over the two month period;
- the overall total number of Greens sold;

and so on.

Activity 37

15 mins

If you've not already done so, follow the steps we've just explained until you have a PivotTable that looks like the one above.

The original question was 'how many products did Alfred sell in total?', but we still can't read this directly from the PivotTable. See if you can find out how to do that. You can get back to the PivotTable Wizard by right clicking anywhere in your PivotTable and choosing **Wizard.**

You should have produced a PivotTable that looks something like this.

Salespers ▾	Month ▾	Data ▾ Sum of Blue	Sum of Green	Sum of All items
Alfred	May	75	125	200
	June	100	200	300
Alfred Total		175	325	500
Bonnie	May	25	75	100
	June	50	100	150
Bonnie Total		75	175	250
Clyde	May	53	97	150
Clyde Total		53	97	150
Grand Total		303	597	900

All you have to do once you have got back to the Wizard and selected **Layout** is drag the **All Items** button into the data area. (We've also moved the Salesperson button into the Row area, because that makes it a bit easier to read, but don't worry if you didn't do that.)

As we said at the outset, this is only a very brief introduction to a very useful tool, but with this basic knowledge you should be able to experiment and learn more using data of your own.

4 Non-numerical information

In the context of *Information in Management* the term **qualitative information** is used to mean any information that is not numerical, but describes or explains things.

4.1 Structure

Another workbook in this series, *Storing and Retrieving Information*, describes how to organize a storage, indexing and information retrieval system in general. Here we are talking about data in individual files or documents.

How can you organize such information? There are several ways, and you could use them alone or in combination.

■ **By name**. In other words, in alphabetical order.

■ **By date**. A date is a sort of number, of course, and information such as correspondence is most usefully organized in strict date order. Dates are also used in a less precise sense, however. For instance, you may organize a list of tasks to be done into those that have to be done by the end of this week, those that must be complete by next Wednesday, and so on.

■ **By category**. This could be anything that items of information have in common with each other, for instance physical items may have a size or colour, staff could be categorized according to department or job title, and so on.

■ **In logical sequence**. Many activities have to be done in a particular order. For instance, if you are making a cup of tea you put water in the kettle and then boil it before pouring it into the cup. That's an obvious example: with more complex work activities it is not always obvious what the most efficient sequence is.

■ **In order of importance**. The most important items of information should be put first: typically these are things that will cost a lot of money, or take up a lot of time, or have a major impact on others.

Activity 38

Here is some information about some of the members of a customer services workteam as at 3 March 2004.

Employee No.	Last name	First name	Position	Date joined	2004 Annual Review
CS0011	Saleem	Khalid	Manager	28/05/1997	28 May
CS0014	Howard	Corinne	Trainee	07/02/2003	Overdue
CS0035	Scott	Carla	Sales assistant	18/04/2002	18 April
CS0073	Bhat	Chandra	Sales assistant	11/02/1999	Overdue
CS0081	Smith	David	Sales assistant	10/10/2002	10 October
CS0094	Otsuka	Dave	Supervisor	08/06/1998	8 June

How is this information organized?

_____

How else might it be organized?

_____

_____

_____

How do you think it should be organized?

_____

_____

_____

The answer to this Activity can be found on page 133.

4.2 Report structure

Not all information can be presented in a list. This book, for instance, is full of information organized into sessions, which in turn are divided into sections, sub-sections, paragraphs, bullet points and activities.

You probably won't be asked to write a book in your job, but you will often have to write some kind of short report on operational matters for your managers to read. You may have to create or update some kind of procedures manual for your own team.

Various techniques can be used to make the content of such a document easy to identify and digest.

- The material in the report should be in a logical order.
- The relative importance of points should be signalled by headings.
- Each point may be numbered in some way to help with cross-reference.
- the document should be easy on the eye, helped by different font sizes, bold, italics, capitals, spacing, and so on.

A typical report structure has the following features.

- **Headings**. There is a hierarchy of headings. There is an overall title and the report as a whole is divided into sections. Within each section main points have a heading in bold capitals, sub-points have a heading in bold, lower-case and sub-sub-points have a heading in italics. (Three levels of headings within a main section is usually considered the maximum number that readers can cope with.) It is better not to underline headings. Underlining makes the page look 'busy' and gets in the way of the content.
- **References**. Sections are lettered A, B, and so on. Main points are numbered 1, 2, and so on, and within each division paragraphs are numbered 1.1, 1.2, 2.1, 2.2. Sub-paragraphs inherit their references from the paragraph above. For instance, the first sub-paragraph under paragraph 1.2 is numbered 1.2.1.
- **Fonts**. Word processors offer you a wealth of fonts these days, but it is best to avoid the temptation. It is often a good idea to put headings in a different font to the main text, but stop there: two fonts is quite enough.

For more information on how to present a report, see *Project and Report Writing* in this series.

Our example is not the only way of organizing a report, of course. You might choose to reference sub-paragraphs 1.2(a), 1.2(b), and so on. You might use roman numerals, although we advise against this. If your report turns out to be longer than you expected and you get up to paragraph XLVIII you are likely to confuse many of your readers unless they happen to be Romans.

The longer the document the better structured it needs to be. Large-scale reports or manuals may run to hundreds of pages, and will therefore require the following.

1. Title page
2. Contents list
3. Objective/term of reference
4. Summary
5. Introduction

6   Main body of the report
7   Conclusions
8   Recommendations
9   Appendices

Appendices are commonly used for:

■   background information that will not be required by all readers;
■   statistical information, which has been abstracted or interpreted in the body of the report;
■   documents referred to in the report.

Activity 39 · 30 mins

Some organizations have what is known as a 'house style' for documents, reports, presentations and similar documents. This is a set of rules that specifies details such as hierarchies of headings, paragraph numbering system, spacing between paragraphs, fonts to use, size and placement of company logo, acceptable colours, and so on.

Develop a 'house style' for your own workteam. The best way to do this is to find an existing document that is five to ten pages long and define a style for each element.

Once you've worked out all the styles you may like to go further and create a word processing template for use in your department. Be sure to save a copy in your Information_in_Management_Session_B folder if you do this.

4.3 Cross-references

Cross-references are pointers to other places in the same document or to other information sources where related information can be found. For instance, if paragraph 3.5 refers to a topic described in more detail later in the document you can save space and avoid repetition by saying 'See paragraph 6.4'.

Activity 40

2 mins

Why is it better to cross-refer to a paragraph number than to a page number?

_____

_____

The answer to this Activity can be found on page 133.

However, ultimately everything is related to everything else and if you are not careful there could be no end to the cross-references. The best advice is to keep them to a minimum, otherwise your readers will be forever flicking from one page to another, and will most likely lose the plot. If too many cross-references seem to be necessary it is probably time to consider re-arranging the information in your report.

4.4 Indexing

An index is an alphabetical list of the names, places and subjects dealt with in a document or book, giving the page or pages on which each item is mentioned.

Shorter documents should not usually need an index if there is good use of headings and a reasonably detailed contents page. If you start to feel that your document will be hard to follow without an index, it may be time to think about re-arranging the material into a more logical structure.

Longer documents – for instance a procedures manual – may well be improved by an index, so let's think about some of the issues.

Your first thought might be to do it by computer. Computers are both a help and a hindrance for indexing. It would be very quick and easy to compile an index listing every occurrence of every word in this session using a word processor. (Such a list is sometimes called a 'concordance'.) But the list would include a massive amount of irrelevant information: words like 'the', 'a', 'it', and so on, which no-one would need to look up.

If you need to prepare an index you need to exercise some discretion. Suppose we wanted to index the occurrences of the word 'spreadsheet' in this session. You can easily do this with a word processor (for example Microsoft Word) by selecting one example of the word and choosing **Insert . . . Index . . . Mark Entry . . . Mark All**.

The result would be something like this (note: these are not the actual page numbers, this is just an example).

Spreadsheet 34, 37, 39, 44, 45, 46, 48, 49, 50, 51, 52, 53, 54, 55, 63

Activity 41

How useful is a list like this to a reader?

Can you suggest how the list might be improved?

It is not very useful at all because most of the references are just examples of where the word 'spreadsheet' is used in passing (for instance in Activities that say something like 'you might find it easier to do this with a spreadsheet'). And it would be very annoying for the reader to have to turn backwards and forwards through a document or book looking at each of 15 instances.

The list would be much improved if it organized the information according to sub-topics that the reader might want to look up, like this.

Spreadsheet
data analysis with, 49
MEDIAN formula, 39, 96
QUARTILE formula, 44, 97

Note that the phrases in our example don't actually appear in the body of this session, so they can't simply be 'tagged' by a word processor.

A good index would also have separate entries under the appropriate letter and topic, for instance as follows.

Data analysis
with spreadsheet, 49

So, although indexing involves a little manipulating of words appearing in a document or set of documents (which computers can do), it involves a lot more of understanding and organizing the ideas and information in the documents, and anticipating the needs of users (which computers cannot do).

Self-assessment 2

10 mins

1 Explain the relationship between information and data.

_____

_____

_____

2 Express these profit and capital figures as ratios with a numerical base of 1. We have worked out the first one for you. It shows that Business A made £1 profit for every £4.73 of capital.

Business	A	B	C	D
Profit	£128,000	£16,250	£3.57 million	£377,500
Capital	£605,000	£16,000	£11.5 million	£9 million
Ratio	1:4.73			

Which business is the most profitable?

_____

3 Here is a series of figures.

4.9 5.1 5.1 5.1 5.3 5.4 5.7 5.9 6.3 6.8 6.8

Find the mean, the median and the mode.

_____

_____

_____

4 ■ The upper quartile is the number that 75% of the values in a set of data are

_____ or equal to.

What are the missing words: 'more than' or 'less than'?

■ The range only uses the middle half of the set of numbers.   True/False?

5 When are PivotTables useful?

_____

_____

6 Name five ways of organizing descriptive information.

_____

7 Besides a good word processor what two other things do you need to prepare a good index?

_____

_____

Answers to these questions can be found on page 126.

5 Summary

- Information is data that has been analysed or processed in some way so as to become meaningful.

- Most business statistics involve simple techniques such as adding, subtracting, multiplying and dividing. For instance, ratios and percentages are both very simple ways of presenting relationships so as to make it easier to compare figures.

- Averages give you an idea of what is typical. The most common type of average is called the arithmetic mean: the total of the numbers divided by the number of values. However, this can sometimes be misleading and two alternatives are the median (the middle value) and the mode (the value that appears most often).

- Grouped data summarizes more detailed figures, for instance you might say that five of the values fall in the range 0 to 10. To perform calculations with such data it is conventional to take the mid-point of each 'class interval', on the assumption that the frequencies occur pretty evenly.

- The spread of data can be measured by looking at the range or percentiles. A percentile is a number that a certain percentage of the values are less than or equal to. However, the most useful figure for statistical analysis is the standard deviation, which is a measure of the amount by which the values in a set of numbers differ from the arithmetic mean.

- Spreadsheets contain a number of tools that help to analyse lists of numerical and/or textual information. Sorting and filtering can be done at the touch of a button. Very complex analysis is possible with a PivotTable.

- Non-numerical lists of information may be organized alphabetically, chronologically, according to some common characteristic, in order of importance, and so on. Longer documents will need to be structured with headings, paragraph numbers and the like.

- Cross-references can save time and avoid repetition but should be kept to a minimum to avoid confusing the reader. Indexes can be useful in longer documents, but the indexer needs to understand the information very well and be able to anticipate the needs of users.

Session C
Presenting information

1 Introduction

Visual presentation of data and statistics has more impact than a block of text or long lists of numbers and is often easier to understand.

We've used various methods of data presentation throughout Sessions A and B of this book without explaining how the data got into that form, or which presentation method to use in different situations.

This final session, therefore, contains a range of advice about the most common methods of visual presentation of data used in business.

You don't have to be a talented artist: everything we describe here can be done using a word processor, a spreadsheet or other sources close to hand.

2 Tables

Tables present data in rows and columns. This form of presentation makes it easier to understand large amounts of data. A railway timetable is a familiar example.

Charing Cross	15:38	16:08	16:18	16:28	16:37	16:45	16:58
Waterloo	15:41	16:11	16:21	16:31	16:40	16:48	17:01
London Bridge	15:49	16:19	16:29	16:39	16:48	16:56	17:09
New Cross	16:01	16:31	16:41	–	17:00	17:08	17:21
Lewisham	16:06	16:36	16:46	16:50	17:05	17:13	17:26

Activity 42

3 mins

You arrive at London Bridge at 16:42 and you want to go to Lewisham. Note down at least three things that this timetable tells you.

_____

_____

_____

_____

There are lots of possible answers: this activity was intended to make you think about the various ways you can use tables. Here are some possibilities.

■ You can look up a specific value by seeing where rows and columns meet. Since you know it is 16:42 you can quickly see from the timetable that your next train is due in six minutes (at 16:48) and will arrive in Lewisham at 17:05.

- You can work your way around the table from your original starting point and test out other scenarios. For instance, you can see that if you had arrived at London Bridge a few minutes earlier you could have got a fast train. If you are not sure that six minutes is long enough to buy a cup of coffee and a bar of chocolate you can get a slightly later train to Lewisham which will give you 14 minutes.
- You can read across rows (or down columns) and compare values. For future reference you can note (by reading right across the London Bridge row) that from 16:19 onwards there is a train to Lewisham roughly every ten minutes.

Tables are a simple way of presenting numerical information. Figures are displayed, and can be compared with each other: relevant totals, subtotals and percentages can also be presented as a summary for analysis.

A table is two-dimensional (rows and columns): so it can only show two variables: a sales analysis for a year, for example, might have rows for months, and columns for products.

SALES FIGURES FOR 2004

	Product A	Product B	Product C	Product D	Total
Jan	370	651	782	899	2,702
Feb	718	312	748	594	2,372
Mar	548	204	585	200	1,537
Apr	382	616	276	359	1,633
May	132	241	184	223	780
Jun	381	216	321	123	1,041
Jul	679	612	733	592	2,616
Aug	116	631	343	271	1,361
Sep	421	661	868	428	2,378
Oct	211	158	653	479	1,501
Nov	306	243	676	404	1,629
Dec	898	759	796	394	2,847
Total	5,162	5,304	6,965	4,966	22,397

You are likely to present data in tabular form very often. Here are the key points to remember.

- The table should have a clear title.
- All columns and rows should be clearly labelled.
- Where appropriate, there should be sub-totals and a right-hand total column for comparison.
- A total figure is often advisable at the bottom of each column of figures also, for comparison. It is usual to double-underline totals at the foot of columns where the table is not presented in a grid.

- Numbers should be right-aligned and they are easier to read if you use the comma separator for thousands.
- Decimal points should line up, either by using a decimal tab or by adding extra zeros (the latter is preferable, in our opinion).

Wrong	Wrong	Right	Right
12.5	12.5	12.5	12.50
13.64	13.64	13.64	13.64
2.9	2.9	2.9	2.90
135	135	135.0	135.00

- A grid or border is optional: see what looks best and is easiest to read (in the above example we've used a grid to illustrate the alignment of numbers more clearly).
- Tables should not be packed with too much data; if you try to get too much in, the information presented will be difficult to read.

2.1 Columns or rows?

Often it will be obvious which information should go in the columns and which should go in rows. Sometimes, it won't matter too much which way round you have the rows and columns. Here are some points to remember.

It is usually easier to read across a short line than a long one. That means that it is usually better to have a long thin table than a short wide one: lots of rows rather than lots of columns. If you had a price list of five hundred products each of which came in three different sizes, you would probably tabulate the information like this, without even considering the other possibility (it wouldn't fit on the paper or screen, anyway, if you had products in columns).

Product	Large	Medium	Small
A001	12.95	11.65	9.35
A002	14.50	12.50	10.50
A003	etc.	etc.	etc.
A004			
A005			
etc.			

However, most people find it easier to compare figures by reading across than by reading down. For example in the previous version of the sales figures it is easier to compare product totals, but in the version below it is easier to compare monthly totals.

	Jan	Feb	Mar	Apr	May	Jun	Jul	Aug	Sep	Oct	Nov	Dec	Total
Product A	370	718	548	382	132	381	679	116	421	211	306	898	5,162
Product B	651	312	204	616	241	216	612	631	661	158	243	759	5,304
Product C	782	748	585	276	184	321	733	343	868	653	676	796	6,965
Product D	899	594	200	359	223	123	592	271	428	479	404	394	4,966
Total	2,702	2,372	1,537	1,633	780	1,041	2,616	1,361	2,378	1,501	1,629	2,847	22,397

If you are not sure what your readers will most want to compare it might be helpful to give them both versions, if practicable.

3 Line graphs

In business, line graphs are usually used to illustrate trends over time of figures such as sales or customer complaints.

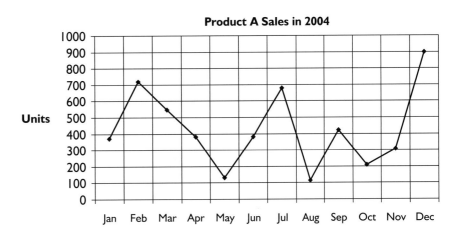

The figures are plotted on a grid and then joined by a line that reflects the 'ups and downs' of the figure, over a period of time. Note that it is conventional to show **time** on the **horizontal axis**.

Now the trend in sales is shown instantly, in a way that is probably not immediately apparent from a column or row of figures. This encourages us to ask questions: for instance why did sales drop in the early months of the year and suddenly shoot up in June and July?

By using different symbols for the plotted points, or preferably by using different colours, several lines can be drawn on a line graph before it gets too overcrowded, and that means that several trends (for example the sales performance of different products) can be compared.

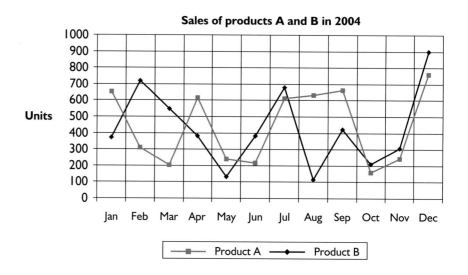

The scale of the vertical axis should be just large enough for you to tell with reasonable accuracy the sales figure at any given point during the period. In the example above we have used a scale of 100 and you can tell, for instance, that sales of product A in April were a little less than 400 (check in the table given in part 2 of this session).

Activity 43

Looking at the graph, what do products A and B have in common?

_____

_____

_____

_____

The answer to this Activity is on page 134.

4 Charts

We'll run through an extended exercise on creating charts without having to get your ruler and crayons out in the next part of this session, but first we'll make some comments in general about the types of chart you are likely to use most often in business reports: bar charts and pie charts.

4.1 Bar charts

The bar chart is one of the most common methods of visual presentation. Data is shown in the form of bars which are the same in width but variable in height. Each bar represents a different item, for example the annual production cost of different products or the number of hours required to produce a product by different workteams.

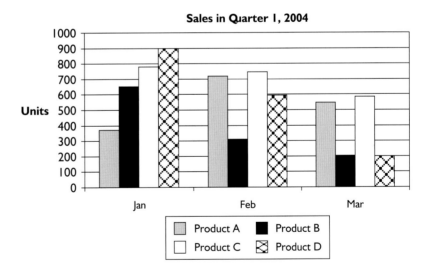

As you can see, here we are more interested in comparing a few individual items in a few individual months (although you can still get a visual impression of trends over time).

Activity 44

Comment on sales of products A and B, based on the chart above.

_____

_____

_____

Our answer to this Activity is on page 134.

Horizontal presentation is also possible.

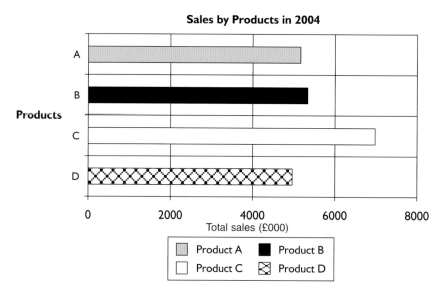

Sales by Products in 2004

There are no hard and fast rules about whether you should use vertical or horizontal presentation. However, these guidelines may help.

- If you are showing trends over time (for instance January to March) vertical bars look best.
- If you are showing differences at a single point in time (the end of 2004, for instance) you might prefer horizontal bars.

4.2 Pie charts

A pie chart shows the relative sizes of the things that make up a total. It is called a pie chart because it is shaped like a pie and is cut into 'slices'.

Pie charts are most effective where the number of slices is small enough to keep the chart simple, and where the difference in the size of the slices is large enough for the eye to judge without too much extra information.

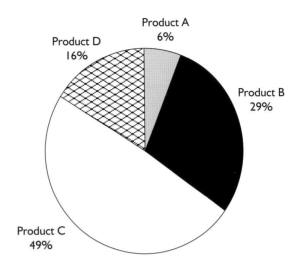

5 How to create charts in Excel

Microsoft Excel has a superb tool for creating hundreds of different charts, graphs and diagrams. We cannot cover all the options in this book, but we will work through the basics for one type of chart. You should then have enough knowledge to be able to experiment on your own.

As we'll see in a moment, the easiest way to create a chart in Excel is to select your data and press F11. However, unless you understand the basics of the Excel Chart Wizard this can often produce unexpected or unwanted results.

Activity 45

30 mins

The whole of this section on charts and Excel is really an extended Activity based on the initial data below.

Create a new folder on your computer with a name such as 'Information_in_ Management_Session_C' and within this create a new spreadsheet file and give it a name such as 'YourName_PerfectTen.xls'.

PERFECT TEN MODEL AGENCY

Perfect Ten is a model agency. Currently it handles the careers of 5 models: Ms White, Ms Red, Ms Green, Ms Yellow and Ms Blue.

Each model is rated each month on a scale of 1 to 10.

Here are the ratings for January to March. You should enter this data in cells A1 to F4 of your spreadsheet and then save your work.

	White	Red	Green	Yellow	Blue
January	10	9	7	8	6
February	10	5	7	3	4
March	10	7	3	2	1

We are going to work on this data to produce a variety of bar charts.

5.1 FII

The quickest way to create a chart in Excel is to use the F11 function key at the top of your keyboard.

- Select cells A1 to F4.
- Press F11.

This will create a chart in a separate spreadsheet called Chart 1.

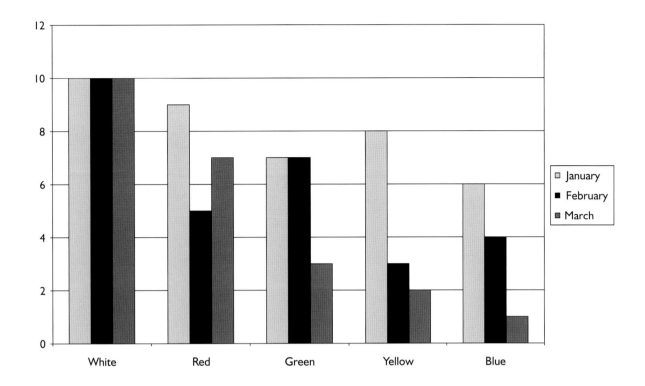

This is quick and easy, but the chances are that this is not how you wanted the chart to look.

To get a bit more control you need to use the Chart Wizard.

5.2 The Chart Wizard

The second quickest way to create a chart in Excel is to use the Chart Wizard. He lives in a little button near the top of the screen.

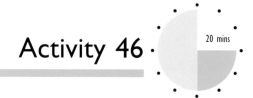

Activity 46

Create a clustered column chart with the model agency data by following these steps.

1   Select cells A1 to F4 again and click on the **Chart Wizard** button. This takes you to 'Step 1' of a four-step process.

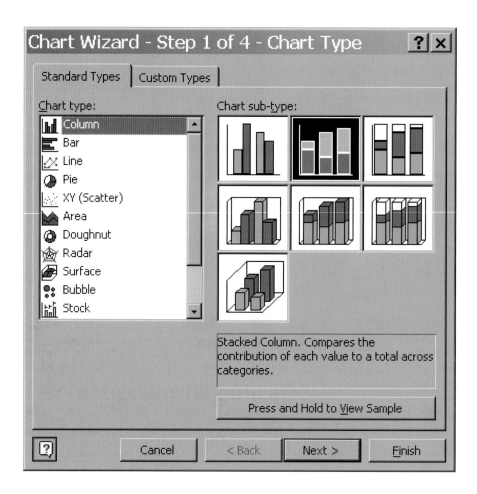

There are all sorts of options here and we will look at several of them, but now we are going to create a column chart of the first sub-type, clustered column.

2   Click on **Next** to go to Step 2.

3   Click **Next** on Step 2 and on Step 3 without making any changes. When you get to step 4 you will see the following options.

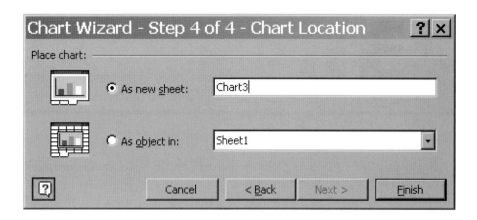

4   We don't want a new sheet this time, so make sure that the chart location is 'As object in Sheet 1' then click on Finish. Your chart will appear on the same page as your data.

Don't forget to save your spreadsheet.

5.3 RelaX!

Your chart should look like this.

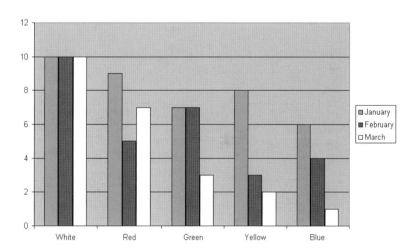

Let's pause to think about how the data has been presented in the charts.

First we need to learn a bit of terminology.

■   The little square box on the right-hand side, containing the words January, February, March, is called the **legend**.
■   The **horizontal** line, labelled White, Red, etc., is called the **X axis**.
■   The **vertical** line, labelled with numbers 0, 2, 4, etc., is called the **Y axis**.

If you find it hard to remember which axis is which just think of the word **relaX**. The X-axis is the one that is having a lie down: in other words X is the horizontal one!

Excel also uses some other names: the X axis is called the **category** axis, and the Y axis is called the **value** axis.

5.4 What goes where?

Here's the data, with the chart underneath.

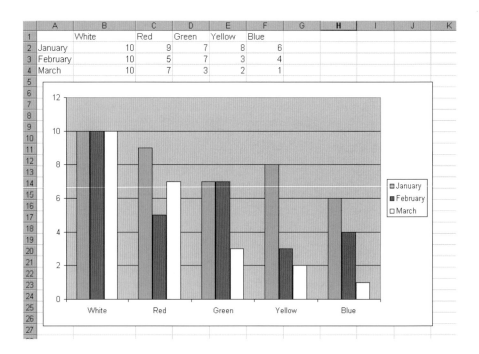

Activity 47 · 5 mins

How do the three elements (legend, X axis, Y axis) relate to the original data?

_____

_____

_____

- The **legend** is derived from the **row labels**.
- The **X axis** is derived from the **column headings**.
- The **Y axis** is derived from the minimum and maximum **numbers** in the body of the table of data.

In fact the default behaviour in Excel is to derive the **X axis** from whatever there is more of, whether they are columns or rows. In this case we have more models than months, so the models go in the X axis. However, you don't have to accept this.

5.5 Changing what goes where

Here's the data and the chart once again.

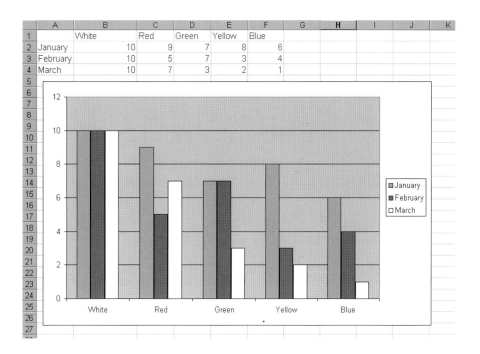

Suppose we wanted the X axis to show the months and the legend to show the girls' names? Do we have to change our original table of data?

The answer is no, of course. Here's how you do it.

I   Right click on a white area of the chart. A menu appears, from which you can choose **Source data**. You will see the following options.

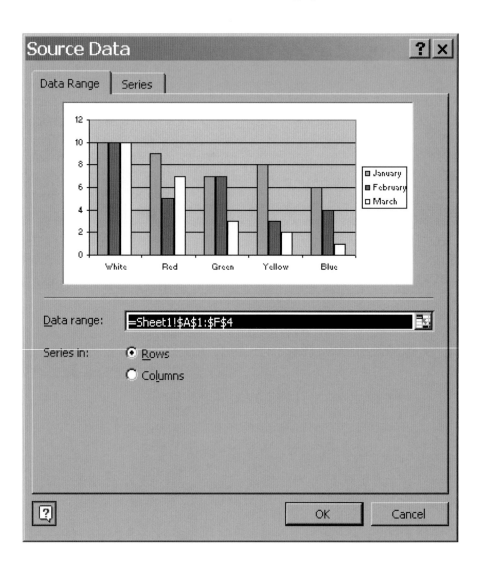

2   The **series** is just another word for what appears in the **legend** box. Select **Columns** and you will immediately see (in the preview shown in your Source data window) that this has done exactly what you wanted: the X axis shows the months; the girls' names (the **column headings**) are in the legend.

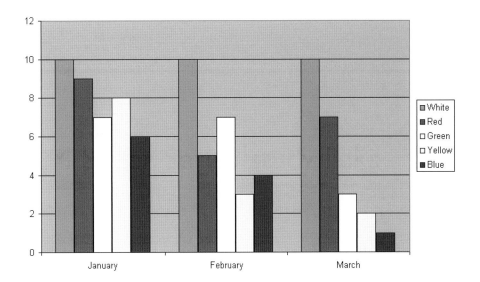

Activity 48   5 mins

Although there isn't space to go into the details, you can do a lot of editing and formatting of your chart after you've created it, simply by right-clicking on it and choosing from the options.

For instance, the bars representing the models will have come out in default colours chosen by Excel, but you can easily change this: right-click on any of the bars representing Ms White, say, and choose **Format data** series from the menu that appears. This gives you the opportunity to change the colour to something more appropriate: white, say.

Try this, and then see what other changes you can make to improve the appearance of your chart.

5.6 Changing the data

Some more information has come in and you need to revise some of your data.

In January, Ms Blue changed her name to Navy.

After reappraisal it has been decided that Ms Navy should have scored 4 in March. And although it is quite unprecedented Ms White scored 11 in February.

	A	B	C	D	E	F
1		White	Red	Green	Yellow	Navy
2	January	10	9	7	8	6
3	February	11	5	7	3	4
4	March	10	7	3	2	4

Activity 49

10 mins

Make the above changes to your original data and watch the effect on the chart. It will update automatically.

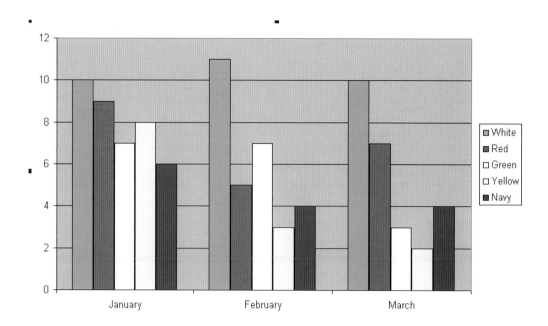

5.7 Other styles of bar charts

You can produce several other types of chart. The instructions below are for a 100% stacked chart on a new sheet within the workbook, using the data we have already created.

1 Select **Sheet 2** and **re-enter the original data**, without any of the changes you've made so far (you could just copy and paste from Sheet 1 and then change the data back to the original values).

2 Highlight cells A1 to F4 and click on the **Chart Wizard** button.

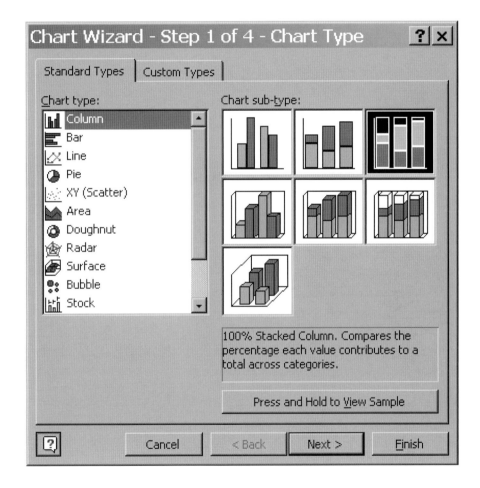

3 Select the **Column** chart type and the **Chart** sub-type, **100% Stacked**, as shown above.

4 Click on **Next** to go to Step 2 of the Wizard. Select the **Series in columns** option.

5 Click on **Next**.

6   At Step 3, Click on **Next** without making any changes.

7   At Step 4 click on **Finish** without making any changes.

The new chart would look like this.

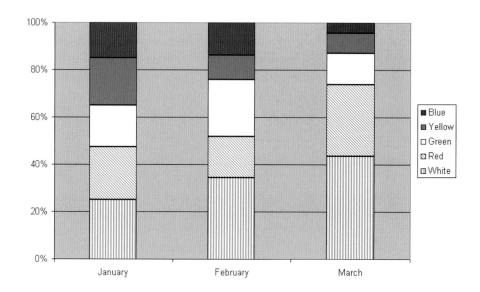

This is all very peculiar. You know, for instance, that Ms White scored a perfect 10 in each month, but here it looks as if her score is getting higher, month after month.

Activity 50

2 mins

Can you explain why it looks as if Ms White's score is getting higher each month?

_____

_____

_____

To make sense of this take a look again at the data.

	A	B White	C Red	D Green	E Yellow	F Blue
1		White	Red	Green	Yellow	Blue
2	January	10	9	7	8	6
3	February	10	5	7	3	4
4	March	10	7	3	2	1

Ms White does indeed score consistently, but the others don't. Most of their scores are getting lower and lower as time goes by. That means that Ms White's score as a percentage of the overall team score gets higher, month by month.

Prove this to yourself. Select cells G2 to G4 and then click on the **AutoSum** button at the top of the page.

Now you can see that Ms White contributed only 25% (10/40) to the overall team score in January, but almost 50% (10/23) in March. And that is exactly what is shown in the chart.

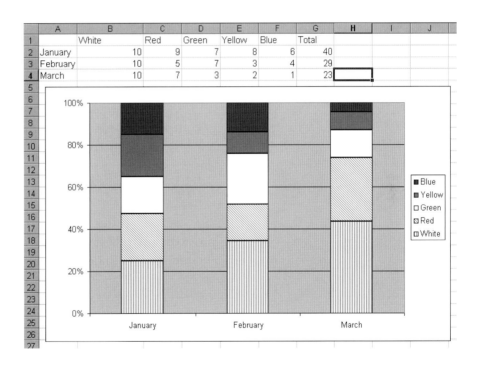

You should now know enough to experiment with charts using some real data of your own. Have a go at creating line graphs and pie charts as well as bar charts.

6 Other types of visual presentation

6.1 Flow charts, organization charts and other labelled diagrams

Flow charts and organization charts are useful ways of presenting and summarizing information that involves a series of steps and choices and/or relationships between the different items.

On the following pages there are some examples of this type of presentation.

If you choose any of these forms of presentation here are some points to bear in mind.

- Be consistent in your use of layout and symbols (and colours, if used). For instance, in our flow chart example a decision symbol is always a diamond with italic text; a YES decision always flows downwards; a NO decision always flows to the right.
- Keep the number of connecting lines to a minimum and avoid lines that 'jump over' each other at all costs.
- Keep the labels or other text brief and simple.
- Hand-drawn diagrams should be as neat and legible as possible. If they are likely to be seen by a lot of people (not just your team) it is better to use a business graphics programme like Microsoft Visio.
- Everyone can draw, but only so well. If you are not expert you can waste an enormous amount of time playing with computer graphics. If it needs to be really beautifully presented and you are not an expert sketch it quickly by hand and then give it to a professional.

A flowchart

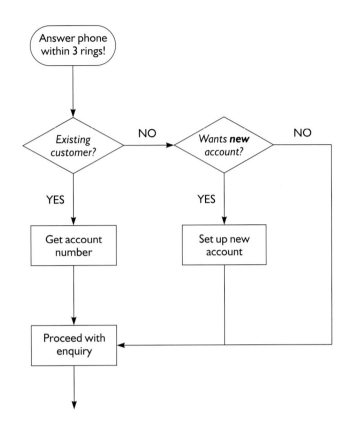

An organization chart

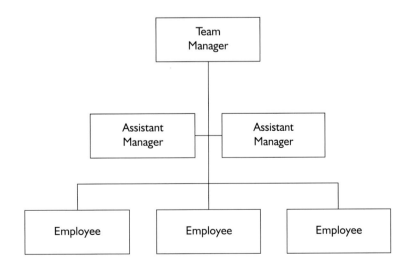

A key point summary

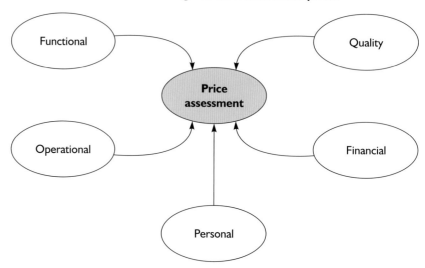

Factors influencing how customers assess prices

Activity 51 · 30 mins

S/NVQ
D1.1, D1.2

This activity may provide the basis of appropriate evidence for your S/NVQ portfolio. If you are intending to take this course of action, either use a computer software program and save the files, or use separate sheets of paper for your answer.

Look at our examples and then create the following charts for your own workteam.

■ An organization chart.
■ A flow chart setting out how to do a work procedure that everybody on your team does regularly.

6.2 Pictograms

A pictogram is a simple graphic image in which the data is represented by a picture or symbol, with a clear key to the items and quantities intended. Different pictures can be used on the same pictogram to represent different elements of the data. For example, a pictogram showing the number of people employed by an organization might use pictures of ... people.

Employees in 2003

Employees in 2004

 *100 male employees*    *100 female employees*

You can see quite easily that the workforce has grown and that the organization employs far more female workers than before.

Pictograms present data in a simple and appealing way. They are often used on television. Watch out for them next time you are watching a news item involving numbers (number of trains late, number of new jobs created, and so on). In pictograms:

- the symbols must be clear and simple;
- there should be a key showing the number that each symbol represents;
- bigger quantities are shown by more symbols, not bigger symbols.

Bear in mind, however, that pictograms are not appropriate if you need to give precise figures. You can use portions of a symbol to represent smaller quantities, but there are limits to what you can do.

 *150 female employees*    *Over 100 employees, mostly male. But how many others and what sex are they?*

6.3 Drawings and graphics

A labelled drawing may sometimes be the best way of presenting a lot of information in a small space. Imagine how difficult it would be to explain all the information you get from the following diagram if you could only use words!

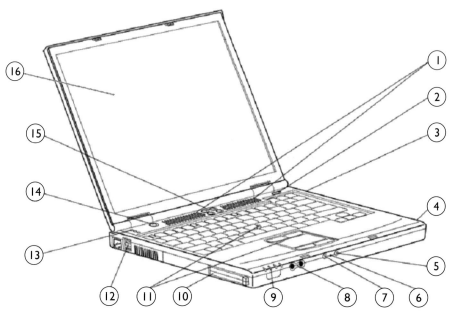

1. Stereo Speakers
2. Power Switch
3. RJ-11 (Modem)
4. Cable Lock Connector
5. Audio-In
6. Microphone
7. Headphone-Out
8. Volume Controls

9. System LEDs
10. PC Card Slots (2)
11. Touchpad + Pointstick
12. USB (2)
13. Keyboard LEDs
14. Suspend Button
15. Easy access Internet Button
16. Colour Display

Activity 52

3 mins

Where might you obtain pictures and graphics such as the pictogram or the computer diagram shown above?

_____

_____

_____

_____

The answer to this Activity is on page 134.

6.4 Maps

Maps can be used to present information which is geographically-based, for example different sales areas.

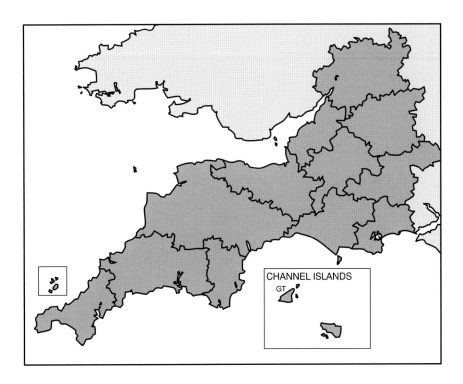

Local road maps or detailed street maps are often sent out to customers who may wish to visit the company's branches, or to people attending a meeting.

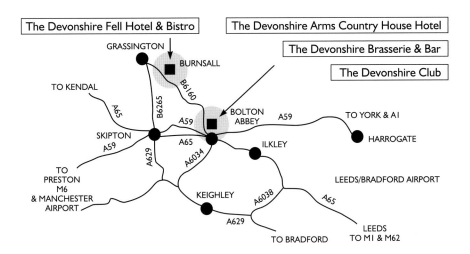

7 Gantt charts and managing projects

A Gantt chart is used to plan the timescale for a project and to organize the resources needed (usually people). (If you remember that a Gantt chart is a sort of 'Time Tracker' you will always get the spelling right: two Ts, not two Ns.)

Gantt charts were developed by Henry Gantt to help with the construction of ships during the First World War but they are more popular than ever today. A Gantt chart is a highly useful visual aid and is also simple to construct and easy to understand. If you have a Year Planner on your wall, you already have a form of Gantt chart.

Gantt charts show the time needed for each activity that makes up a project as a horizontal bar starting at the appropriate day, week or month of the project plan.

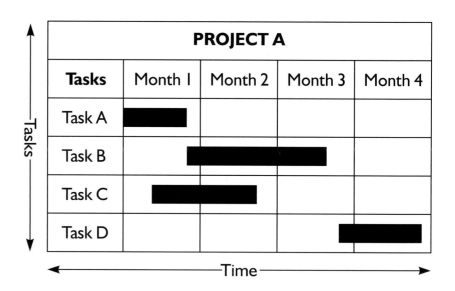

In this project we can see from the chart that we have to wait until task A is finished before we start task B, but task C can overlap to some extent with tasks A and B.

Activity 53

2 mins

What else does this Gantt chart tell you about Tasks C and D?

_____

_____

_____

You can see from the chart that you could probably delay the start of task C until about the middle of month 2 without delaying the project as a whole. However, task D cannot be started until task B is complete.

A useful addition to a Gantt chart is to use **planned** and **actual bars**, like this.

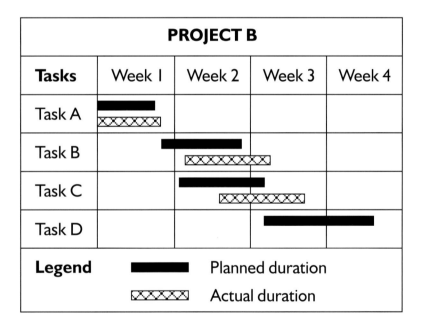

PROJECT B				
Tasks	Week 1	Week 2	Week 3	Week 4
Task A	██████			
Task B		██████		
Task C		██████		
Task D			████████	

Legend	████████ Planned duration
	✕✕✕✕✕✕ Actual duration

Activity 54

3 mins

Interpret the chart for project B, commenting on each of the tasks and the relationships between them. Assume that it is now the Thursday of week 3.

The answer to this Activity can be found on page 134.

7.1 Gantt charts, software and managing resources

If your work involves a great deal of project management (one-off, fairly lengthy jobs, as opposed to a predictable daily routine) you will probably use specialist project management software such as Microsoft Project, which has all sorts of aids and charting tools built in, including the ability to create and update Gantt charts at the touch of a button. There are also specialist business graphics programs like Microsoft Visio that make it very easy to create complex Gantt charts.

Microsoft Excel does not have any built-in features devoted to project management. But that's not going to stop us using it to illustrate how helpful Gantt charts can be when it comes to managing the people and resources under your management.

Let's suppose you manage a multi-skilled workteam of 20 people, each capable of working on any of the tasks. Your team's next project involves seven tasks which you have codenamed A to G.

- Task A will take five days and require 12 people.
- Task B will take five days and require six people.
- Task C cannot be started until task B is complete. It will take two days and require eight people.

- Task D, which can only be done when task A is complete, will need four people and will take one day.
- Task E, which also has to wait for task A to be finished, will take seven days and will need 10 people to work on it
- Task F cannot be started until task D is complete. It will take three days and it will need 12 workers.
- Task G will take three days but can only be done when both task C and task E are complete.

Activity 55

5 mins

Arrange this information in a table and then calculate the maximum number days that the project could take. Can you think of any way of doing the project in a shorter time?

If you add up the number of days for each task you will find that it comes to 26 days. However, you can make it shorter by doing some tasks at the same time. For instance, tasks A and B only require 18 staff in total so they can be done at the same time, shaving 5 days off the total amount of time required.

Here is the table.

Task	Preceded by	Days	People
A	–	5	12
B	–	5	6
C	B	2	8
D	A	1	8
E	A	7	10
F	D	3	12
G	C, E	3	6

You could work through all the rest of the data as we did above seeing where you could do tasks concurrently to shorten the project, but the quickest way is to draw a network diagram such as the one shown overleaf (project management software would produce one of these for you automatically).

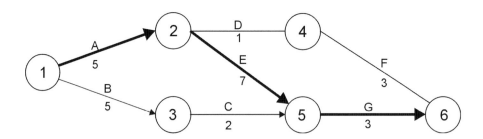

Compare this with the information in the table to make sure you understand it. Next we add up the days on each of the paths.

ADF = 5 + 1 + 3 = 9 days

AEG = 5 + 7 + 3 = 15 days

BCG = 5 + 2 + 3 = 10 days

The thick line, path AEG, is known as the **critical path** because it is the longest path through the network. Nonetheless, the critical path represents the shortest amount of time to complete the project, assuming that there are no resource constraints.

However, we know that we only have 20 people available, so let's now draw a Gantt chart with one bar for the critical path and further bars for the remaining tasks that depend on each other. We've done this using a spreadsheet, as follows.

	A	B	C	D	E	F	G	H	I	J	K	L	M	N	O	P
1	Days	1	2	3	4	5	6	7	8	9	10	11	12	13	14	15
2	AEG	Task A					Task E							Task G		
3	People	12	12	12	12	12	10	10	10	10	10	10	10	6	6	6
4																
5	BC	Task B					Task C									
6	People	6	6	6	6	6	8	8								
7																
8	DF				Task D	Task F										
9	People				8	12	12	12								
10																
11	Total people	18	18	18	26	30	30	30	10	10	10	10	10	6	6	6

You can use a formula such as =SUM(B2:B10) in cell B11: the spreadsheet will simply ignore any information that is not a number.

From this we can see that on days 4 to 7 we are trying to do too much: we only have 20 staff but we are trying to do the work of between 26 and 30 people. This either means lots of overtime, or you will need to find another solution.

Activity 56 · 5 mins

Set up a spreadsheet exactly as shown above. Can you use it to devise a better solution?

Don't forget to save your spreadsheet.

_____

_____

_____

If you look at the Gantt chart the solution should be obvious. For instance, if you select the DF bar (cells E8:H9) and drag it to the right so that it occupies cells I8:L9 you have partially solved the problem. Only days 9 to 11 will then need more people (22) than you have available.

If you drag the DF bar a little further so that it occupies cells M8 to P9 you solve the problem completely.

	A	B	C	D	E	F	G	H	I	J	K	L	M	N	O	P
1	Days	1	2	3	4	5	6	7	8	9	10	11	12	13	14	15
2	AEG	Task A					Task E							Task G		
3	People	12	12	12	12	12	10	10	10	10	10	10	10	6	6	6
4																	
5	BC	Task B					Task C										
6	People	6	6	6	6	6	8	8									
7																	
8	DF													Task D	Task F		
9	People													8	12	12	12
10																	
11	Total people	18	18	18	18	18	18	18	10	10	10	10	18	18	18	18

What we have done is to use up the spare time we had on days 8 to 15 on 'non-critical' tasks. We have deferred the start of tasks D and F until the latest possible days. This also gives us a little bit of breathing space (spare resources) on days 8 to 11, which might be handy if any of the earlier tasks take longer than expected.

Self-assessment 3

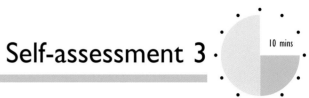

10 mins

1 Fill in the missing words using words from this list.

long, right; short; thin; wide.

Numbers in a table should be _____-aligned. It is usually better to

have a _____ _____ table than a _____

_____ table.

2 Create a line graph (either by hand or by using a spreadsheet) based on the following information.

Units	Production cost
0	0
10	1,000
20	1,400
30	1,450
40	1,475
50	2,600

■ What does your graph show you?

_____

_____

_____

■ A pie chart would be a better way of showing this data. True/False.

3 When you create a chart using Excel the horizontal axis (also known as the X/Y* axis or category/value/series* axis) is derived from:

■ row labels
■ column headings
■ either rows or column headings

depending on the situation*.

(*Delete as applicable.)

4   If you wanted to create a graphical representation of the steps involved in a regular procedure carried out by your organization what is the best type of chart to use?

   a   A Gantt chart.
   b   An organization chart.
   c   A flow chart.
   d   A pictogram.

_____

5   In a project planning network diagram, is the critical path the longest or the shortest path?

6   A project will definitely take longer than expected if:

   a   any individual task takes longer than expected;
   b   a non-critical task takes longer than expected;
   c   a critical task takes longer than expected.

Answers to these questions can be found on page 127.

8 Summary

- Tables are a simple way of presenting numerical and/or textual information. Figures are displayed, and can be compared with each other: relevant totals, subtotals, percentages can also be presented as a summary for analysis. Clear labels and headings and proper alignment are issues to consider.

- Line graphs are usually used to illustrate trends over time of figures such as sales. It is conventional to show time on the horizontal axis. Line graphs can help draw attention to questions that need to be asked and (within limits) can be used to compare performance.

- In a bar chart, data is shown in the form of vertical or horizontal bars which are the same in width but variable in height. Each bar represents a different item, so bar charts are generally more useful than graphs for comparisons.

- A pie chart is useful if you want to show the relative sizes of the things that make up a total.

- A large variety of charts and diagrams can be generated by the charting tools in spreadsheet programs such as Microsoft Excel.

- Other types of visual presentation used in business include organization charts, flow charts, pictograms, drawings or other graphics and maps.

- Gantt charts are used to plan the timescale for a project and perhaps to organize the resources needed (usually people). Gantt charts show the time needed for each activity that makes up a project as a horizontal bar starting at the appropriate day, week or month of the project plan.

Performance checks

1 Quick quiz

Jot down the answers to the following questions on *Information in Management*.

Question 1   There are differences between the information used by top management and the information used by managers lower down the organization. Write a brief summary of the differences.

Question 2   Collecting more and more information can result in diminishing returns. Why?

Question 3   When sorting through piles of paperwork to look for relevant information what is the first thing you should do?

Question 4   Give five examples of mathematical models used in business.

Question 5   Give a brief summary of the technique you might use if you had to choose how best to allocate resources such as staff time between two tasks.

_____

_____

Question 6   What do we mean by 'raw data'?

_____

_____

Question 7   A school delivers 2,357 pupil-hours of teaching per year. In 2002 it did this with a staffing level of 15; in 2003 the figure was 14. What were the pupil-hours per head for the two years?

2002_____

2003_____

Question 8   Why is the arithmetic mean sometimes misleading?

_____

_____

Question 9   How can you estimate an average when you only have grouped data, such as '53 people in the survey were aged between 19 and 25'?

_____

_____

Question 10   If you know the standard deviation of a set of numbers what two things can you say about the set of numbers as a whole?

_____

_____

Question 11   Within a long document how should headings and paragraphs be organized?

_____

_____

Question 12   What are the key points to remember when presenting numbers in a table?

_____

_____

Question 13 The manually produced bar chart below has been incorrectly drawn. What is wrong with it?

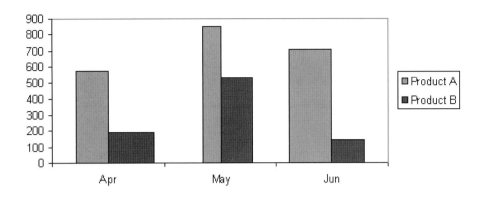

Question 14 How can you edit and/or format an Excel chart after you have created it?

Question 15 Give one advantage and one disadvantage of a pictogram.

Answers to these questions can be found on pages 134–136.

2 Workbook assessment

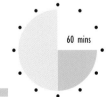

60 mins

The following information was derived from the website of the Office of National Statistics. The figures represent millions of pounds spent on various consumer items in the UK: for instance, in 1998 UK households spent a total of £31,656,000 on clothing and footwear. The figures are correct, although we have not laid out the table very well.

Ideally you should use a spreadsheet to do this assessment. If you do, make sure you save your spreadsheet file.

	1998	1999	Total 1998 to 2001	2000	2001
Clothing and footwear	31656	33661	143826	36969	41540
Housing, water, electricity, gas & other fuels	22418	22134	90621	22953	23116
Furnishings, hsehld eqpt & routine hse mntnce	26933	28456	118931	30866	32676
Health	3872	3831	15299	3811	3785
Transport	43659	44864	184776	46333	49920
Communication	532	708	2928	804	884
Recreation and culture	42503	48861	208095	55549	61182
Miscellaneous goods and services	12635	12924	53366	13701	14106
Alcoholic beverages, tobacco and narcotics	19553	20203	80091	20164	20171
Food and non-alcoholic beverages	52983	54102	218830	55610	56135

- Prepare your own version of the table, paying careful attention to layout and presentation issues. Before you start, make sure you read all the other requirements below, in case they affect your layout choices, especially if you are **not** doing this assessment using a spreadsheet.
- Make sure you have entered all the figures correctly. You can use the total column as a check that you have entered the figures correctly.
- Add further totals or sub-totals wherever you think they may be helpful.
- Pick two categories of expenditure and prepare bar charts, pie charts, graphs or other graphical illustrations, as you think appropriate, to make the information easier to understand. Write brief notes to accompany each chart or graphic you prepare, explaining what it shows.
- Analyse the figures in a way that shows how much each category contributed to total consumer expenditure in each year and comment on any trends you notice.
- Based on the trends you have noticed, but without doing any further calculations predict annual expenditure for each category in 2002.
- Calculate the average percentage change in expenditure between 1998 and 2001 and redo your prediction for 2002 using the average annual increase or decrease.
- Estimate (very roughly) how much you personally spend per year in each of the categories. How does your own consumer expenditure compare with the national figures?

60 mins

3 Work-based assignment

S/NVQ
D1.1, D1.2

The time guide for this assignment gives you an approximate idea of how long it is likely to take you to write up your findings. You will find you need to spend some additional time gathering information, talking to colleagues, and thinking about the assignment.

Your written response to this assignment could form the basis of useful evidence for your S/NVQ portfolio. The assignment is designed to help you demonstrate the following Personal Competences:

- communicating;
- searching for information.

What you have to do

Your task is to carry out an 'audit' of your role in the information network in your organization, and it is in two parts:

- first, listing all the information you generate and supply in various directions;
- then considering what you could do to improve the way you handle these information flows.

1 Listing the information

Produce your list as a table like this.

No.	What information?	For whom?	When?	For what purpose?
A	SUPPLIED UPWARDS (to more senior management)			
	1			
	2 etc.			
B	SUPPLIED DOWNWARDS (to workteam)			
	1			
	2 etc.			
C	SUPPLIED OUTWARDS (to suppliers, colleagues, customers etc.)			
	1			
	2 etc.			

You may want to consult colleagues and your workteam to make sure your list is complete. Make sure that you don't just write 'for information' in the 'For what purpose?' column – you need to specify what purpose the information is (or should be) used for.

2 Reviewing your information output

Now review your list and think about ways in which you could be providing **better** information in a **better way**. This may involve:

- producing it in a more timely way;
- making it more comprehensible;
- summarizing key points more clearly;
- using different ways to present the key points (e.g. graphics);
- improving the standard of presentation.

a Comment on the general standard and quality of the information that you generate. What in general could you do to make it more effective in conveying the key messages and more useful for the people who receive it?

b Identify **two** specific items of information that you could improve and write detailed notes on what you would do and how.

This is an important and relevant exercise. Organizations live on information, and better quality information makes them function better. Individuals who can communicate important information better make better managers, and have better career prospects. Complete this assignment thoroughly and put your improvements into practice: you and your organization will both feel the benefit.

Reflect and review

1 Reflect and review

Now that you have completed your work on *Information in Management*, it is time to review what you have leant in relation to the objectives that we set at the beginning. Using information in management is a very big subject, and what you have learned will be only the beginning. Information in one aspect or another – getting it, sorting it analysing it, compiling it, sending it – increasingly dominates management life, and you will encounter it in many forms. Some of this will be new as technology, systems and expert software continue to develop.

Even so, what you have learned should have put you well on the way to fulfilling the objectives set out at the beginning of this book.

Here is the first objective.

■ Understand the need to collect information relevant to decisions.

Whenever you are collecting information you should ask yourself questions. Here are some examples.

- Is it accurate?
- Is it relevant?
- Are the sources reliable?
- Does it provide a guide to the future?
- What does it mean?
- How can it be used?

This is partly about understanding information in context, but it is also about being critical. You shouldn't necessarily take things at their face value.

■ Think about some information that you have recently received. This might be an unsolicited mail shot, a regular newsletter that you subscribe to or information that you have specifically requested or sought out on the Internet.

■ What critical questions could you ask?

_____

_____

_____

The next objective was the first of several relating to the use of information once you have collected it.

■ Use decision-making models.

A decision-making model takes some of the pain out of information analysis because it is a tried and trusted technique. You don't have to think too hard about how to analyse the problem, you simply have to plug the numbers into a formula and see what the result is.

There is a wide range of decision-making models – we only looked at a few of the best known ones in this book, particularly stock-related calculations, resource allocation problems and 'what if' scenarios. You may use some kind of model in your work without even realizing it, for example if you or someone else in your department has a devised a spreadsheet to quickly calculate the answer to a routine problem, or if you have some kind of specialized software, either part of the accounting system or a stand-alone package.

■ What decision-making models do you have to help you with routine decisions that arise in your own work? Have you identified any routine problems that could be dealt with more quickly and effectively if you took the time to develop a spreadsheet solution?

_____

_____

_____

_____

The next objectives relate to less routine situations: you have a mass of data, but no predefined way of understanding and summarizing what it all means.

- Analyse numerical data.

- Use statistics to enhance understanding of information.

We tried to reassure you that numerical analysis in business frequently involves no more than finding totals and calculating percentages or ratios. Often the question you need to ask is 'what is typical?', and you now know about a selection of averages that you can calculate and the importance of considering the range of the values.

These techniques are valuable in a large variety of operational management situations, for instance when you need to know how the individuals in your team are performing, if you need to set targets, if you want to find out who is the best supplier of a product or service, or if you need to forecast figures, say for budgeting.

- Think about how you could make more use of simple statistics in your work. Note down some examples of problems that you currently deal with on the basis of 'gut-feeling' or intuition. Would you make better decisions if you took more time to analyse the numbers?

Not all the information you have to deal with is numerical, of course, and this was reflected in our next objective.

- Analyse qualitative information.

Initial analysis will probably involve sorting the information in some way: by date or by category or alphabetically and so on. And because there is often no 'one best way' of sorting qualitative information it is well worth getting familiar with the sorting facilities that are available in software packages such as Excel with its filters and other tools.

Subsequent analysis of qualitative information, and analysis of information that does not naturally go into a simple list will require report writing skills: how to use a hierarchy of headers, section and paragraph numbering and so on to make it easy for readers to find the information they need at a glance; when (and when not) to include cross-references.

- Think about some of the reports or other information that you have to generate for others to read. Note down three or four things that you could start doing now to make them work better for your readers.

_____

_____

_____

_____

- Some of the improvements you would like may involve developing new skills. Make a note of these.

_____

_____

The next objectives also concerned the presentation of information.

- Select the most appropriate way to present statistical information.
- Present charts and diagrams effectively.
- Interpret statistical information from tables, charts or diagrams.

Sometimes it is enough to present the information in a simple table, as long as you remember all the rules about headings and alignment and totals. Charts and diagrams can be very useful ways of summarizing information and showing up trends that may not be apparent if all you have is a mass of figures. The most commonly used types in business are graphs, bar charts and pie charts.

The best way to create a business chart is to use a spreadsheet charting tool. This is very easy in theory but needs a little practice to get the data exactly as you want it. That raises another issue: you should of course be able to explain in words what your charts mean.

- Get into the habit of summarizing your data in the form of charts and graphs. You may not always use the charts you create in your final report but they are quick and easy to create if you use the right tools and they may draw attention to trends that would otherwise go unnoticed.

  Make a note of any charts that you could produce regularly to illustrate your team's current performance and performance targets.

_____

_____

_____

_____

The final objective listed at the beginning of this book was this.

■ Use spreadsheets and spreadsheet databases

Of course this is not a skill to be developed in isolation, but in the context of all the other objectives above. Spreadsheets offer you a huge number of time-saving tools and techniques for manipulating and analysing data, especially (but not only) numerical data. If you or members of your team are still analysing figures using pen, paper and calculator you are almost certainly wasting your time.

■ Do you know how to extract data from other computer systems used in your organization into a spreadsheet, for further analysis? Find out how to do so, if not, and make a note of any ways you think it would help you to have information in a more easily analysable form.

_____

_____

_____

_____

■ Do all the members of your team have adequate training in the use of spreadsheets (and other office software)? Make a note of any training needs that you have identified, both for yourself and for your team members.

_____

_____

_____

_____

2 Action plan

Use this plan to further develop for yourself a course of action you want to take. Make a note in the left-hand column of the issues or problems you want to tackle, and then decide what you intend to do, and make a note in column 2.

The resources you need might include time, materials, information or money. You may need to negotiate for some of them, but they could be something easily acquired, like half an hour of somebody's time, or a chapter of a book. Put whatever you need in column 3. No plan means anything without a timescale, so put a realistic target completion date in column 4.

Finally, describe the outcome you want to achieve as a result of this plan, whether it is for your own benefit or advancement, or a more efficient way of doing things.

Desired outcomes

1 Issues	2 Action	3 Resources	4 Target completion

Actual outcomes

3 Extensions

Extension 1	Book	*Managing Information and Statistics*
	Authors	Roland Bee, Frances Bee
	Edition	May 1999
	Publisher	Chartered Institute of Personnel and Development (CIPD)
	ISBN	0852927851

Extension 2	Book	*Statistics for the Utterly Confused*
	Author	Lloyd R Jaisingh
	Edition	May, 2000
	Publisher	McGraw-Hill
	ISBN	0071350055

Extension 3	Book	*Excel 2002 for Dummies*
	Author	Greg Harvey
	Edition	July, 2001
	Publisher	Hungry Minds Inc
	ISBN	0764508229

4 Answers to self-assessment questions

Self-assessment 1 on page 32

1 Statement a is incorrect; the job of top managers is to manage the strategy and general direction of the organization. It is not to get involved in every detail of operations. This is the job of middle managers and first line managers, who can be asked to report upwards when necessary.

Statement b is correct. For example, a maintenance workteam doesn't **need** to know about what kind of sales techniques are currently being brought in.

Yet experience and research both show that keeping people in the picture makes them feel part of the wider organization, and helps improves morale and motivation.

2   Here are the six stages.

- Stage 1: Problem recognition.
- Stage 2: Problem definition and structuring.
- Stage 3: Identifying alternative courses of action.
- Stage 4: Making and communicating the decision.
- Stage 5: Implementing the decision.
- Stage 6: Review of the effects of the decision.

3   The paragraph should read as follows.

We need information **to make decisions** [PHRASE C], but usually **we don't have enough** [PHRASE E] information to make good decisions. That means **acquiring more information** [PHRASE D], but too much information **creates problems in itself** [PHRASE A], because the costs of **obtaining, sorting and evaluating** [PHRASE B] it can be greater than its value.

4   ■ Step 1: Find out which resource is the limiting factor.
   ■ Step 2: Identify the gross profit earned by each product per unit of the scarce resource.
   ■ Step 3: Work out the production budget, making enough of the product with the highest gross profit per limiting factor to meet the full sales demand, and using the remaining units of scarce resource to make as many as possible of the other product(s) in order of profitability per unit of scarce resource.

5   A business decision model usually represents a real-life situation in terms of **mathematical relationships and formulae**. The model will consist of **several interrelated variables**. A model allows you to try out **different scenarios** to see **which course of action gives the best results**.

6   The probability of someone being absent is $23/260 = 0.089$. The full number of hours that should be available is $22 \times 7 \times 10 = 1,540$. The expected hours lost are therefore $0.088 \times 1,540 =$ about 136. The expected hours available are $1,540 - 136 = 1,404$. You may have got a slightly different answer, depending on rounding.

7   When drawing a decision tree a **circle** is used as the symbol for **an outcome point**, and a **square** is used as the symbol for a decision point. The branches from **an outcome point** have probabilities assigned to them. A decision tree is evaluated from **right** to left.

Reflect and review

1   Information is data that has been analysed or processed in some way so as to become meaningful. For instance, data might be organized into a table with column headings and labels.

2   The ratios are as follows.

		Business		
	A	**B**	**C**	**D**
profit	£128,000	£16,250	£3.57 million	£377,500
capital	£605,000	£16,000	£11.5 million	£9 million
ratio:	1:4.73	1:0.98	1:3.22	1:23.84

Business B is the most profitable: it makes a profit of £1 for every 97p invested.

3   In this series of 11 numbers:

- the mean is 62.4/11 = 5.67
- the median is the middle number in the series: 5.4
- the mode is the number that appears most frequently: 5.1.

4   ■ The upper quartile is the number that 75% of the values in a set of data are less than or equal to.

■ The range uses the highest and lowest values from the whole of the data. The inter-quartile range is the difference between the values of the upper and lower quartiles and hence shows the range of values of the middle half of the set of data. So the statement is false.

5   PivotTables are useful when there are several different ways to analyse the data, for instance when there are several different categories corresponding to the same figures (for example sales per salesperson per month).

6   By name, by date, by category, in logical sequence and by order of importance.

7   A good understanding of the ideas and information in the documents, and an ability to anticipate the needs of users.

Self-assessment 3 on page 108

1   Numbers in a table should be **RIGHT**-aligned. It is usually better to have a **LONG THIN** table than a **SHORT WIDE** table.

2   This is our graph, produced with Microsoft Excel.

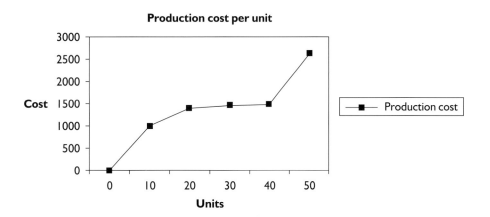

The graph clearly shows that production costs per unit gradually fall up to the level of 40 units, but then rise dramatically if more than 40 units are produced. This would probably be because one person or one machine could produce no more than 40 units: if you wanted 50 you would have to get a second person or machine.

A pie chart would be quite unsuitable for this sort of data. A bar chart would show it equally well, however.

3   When you create a chart using Excel the horizontal axis (also known as the **X** axis or **CATEGORY** axis) is derived from: **EITHER ROW LABELS OR COLUMN HEADINGS, DEPENDING ON THE SITUATION**.

By default the horizontal axis is derived from whatever there are more of, rows or columns, but you can choose yourself, either when you are creating the chart, or after you have created it.

4   c   A flow chart is best because this is a regular procedure.

5   In a project planning network diagram the critical path is the longest path.

6   c is the correct answer. However, a project may also take longer than expected if a non-critical task is delayed, but this is not inevitable.

5 Answers to activities

Activity 7
on page 12

Graph B signifies that the value of the extra information is directly proportional to its cost on a 1:1 ratio. In graph C, the value of the extra information actually grows steadily as more is obtained. Both these scenarios are quite unrealistic.

The graph that correctly describes the situation is graph A. This shows that, to begin with, more information means rapidly rising value. However, the graph line soon flattens out, and the value of each extra bit of information soon declines to almost nil.

Activity 9
on page 16

Input variables: £3,000; 70%.
Output variables: 2100.
Controlled variables: £3,000.
Non-controlled variables: £2,100.

In this case the answer will always be £2,100. If your ideal monthly salary were £30,000 you would only achieve 7% of that.

Activity 11
on page 21

In this example there are two potential limiting factors, labour hours and materials. To make things a bit easier we left most of the other numbers the same and, as long as you spotted this, you know that the labour hours needed = 27,000 hours: there is no shortfall there.

Let's look at materials.

	Product 1	**Product 2**	**Total**
Materials per unit	4	5	
Sales demand	8,000 units	11,000 units	
Materials needed	32,000	55,000	87,000
Materials available			70,000
Shortfall			17,000

Materials are a limiting factor: there is a shortfall of 17,000 units.

The second step is to identify the gross profit earned by each product per unit of the scarce resource, that is, per unit of material.

	Product 1	Product 2
	£	£
Sales price	60	50
Variable cost	44	40
Unit gross profit	16	10
Materials per unit	4	5
Gross profit per unit of materials	£4	£2

This time it is more profitable to make product 1 than product 2.

Product	Demand	Materials required	Materials available	Priority for manufacture
Product 1	8,000	32,000	32,000	1st
Product 2	11,000	55,000	38,000 (balance)	2nd
		87,000	70,000	

Product	Units	Materials needed	Gross profit	Total
			£	
Product 1	8,000	32,000	16	128,000
Product 2 (balance)	7,600	38,000	10	76,000
		70,000		204,000
Less fixed costs				50,000
Profit				154,000

The balance is calculated by dividing the number of remaining units of material by the number of units of material needed to make a product 2: 38,000/5 = 7,600.

**Activity 12
on page 23**

Here are all the formulae. To see yours like this press **Control +** ` (the key just above the Tab key) and to get the numbers back again press **Control +** ` again. You may want to print it out in formula form, to show that you have done this Activity, and print out the numbers versions when you are doing the 'what if' analysis.

	A	B	C	D	E
1			Month 1	Month 2	Month 3
2	Sales	1.2	5000	=C2*$B$2	=D2*$B$2
3	Cost of sales	0.65	=-C2*$B$3	=-D2*$B$3	=-E2*$B$3
4	Gross profit		=SUM(C2:C3)	=SUM(D2:D3)	=SUM(E2:E3)
5					
6	**Receipts**				
7	Current month	0.6	=C2*$B$7	=D2*$B$7	=E2*$B$7
8	1 month in arrears	0.4		=C2*$B$8	=D2*$B$8
9	2 months in arrears	0			=C2*$B$9
10			=SUM(C7:C9)	=SUM(D7:D9)	=SUM(E7:E9)
11	**Payments**		=C3	=D3	=E3
12			=SUM(C10:C11)	=SUM(D10:D11)	=SUM(E10:E11)
13	Bank balance b/fwd		0	=C14	=D14
14	Bank balance c/fwd		=SUM(C12:C13)	=SUM(D12:D13)	=SUM(E12:E13)

If the cost of sales is 68%, the bank balance at the end of Month 3 is £2,944. Remember to change the figure back to 65% before doing the next part.

If the payment pattern changes, the bank balance at the end of Month 3 will be £1,450. Again, remember to restore the original figures.

If sales growth is only 15%, the bank balance at the end of Month 3 will be £3,432.

**Activity 17
on page 31**

The EV at point E will be £63,060, so the decision at point C is the same.

Sales	£		£
High	140,000	0.24	33,600
Medium	78,000	0.55	42,900
Low	−64,000	0.21	−13,440
			63,060

The EV at point B will be as follows.

			EV
	£		£
Point C	63,060	0.75	47,295
Point D	16,000	0.25	4,000
			51,295

Taking away the test marketing cost of £32,000 gives us £19,295, so the decision will still be to test market the product.

**Activity 19
on page 37**

It would be better if the data were organized in alphabetical order of country, not numerical order. (This would be more obvious if you saw the a list with hundreds of codes.)

**Activity 21
on page 39**

Company	Capital employed (£m)	2004 profit (£)	Capital:profit ratio	Profit %
A	15.80	995,400	1:63,000	6.3%
B	5.90	324,500	1:55,000	5.5%
C	44.20	5,348,200	1:121,000	12.1%
D	21.40	2,461,000	1:115,000	11.5%
E	0.85	79,000	1:92,941	9.3%
F	87.00	13,746,000	1:158,000	15.8%

Most profitable: Company F.

Least profitable: Company B.

**Activity 22
on page 42**

Period	1	2	3	4	5	Average
Data						
Output (units)	217.0	221.0	229.0	214.0	233.0	222.80
Headcount	61.0	61.0	59.0	51.0	51.0	56.60
Cost (£'000s)	119.6	125.3	125.1	119.5	131.3	124.16
Hours worked	2,318.0	2,379.0	2,315.0	2,116.0	2,167.0	2,259.00
Indexes						
Output per head	3.56	3.62	3.88	4.20	4.57	3.97
Cost per unit of output	0.55	0.57	0.55	0.56	0.56	0.56
Hours worked per unit	10.68	10.76	10.11	9.89	9.30	10.15
Cost per head	1.96	2.05	2.12	2.34	2.57	2.21

We have an example here of an organization that is trying to achieve higher productivity, but failing to make real gains.

Productivity, in the form of output per head and the hours needed to produce each unit, has improved considerably. Unfortunately, the labour cost per head has risen, so the cost per unit – the key issue for competitiveness – has remained the same. The aim of improving productivity is to reduce costs in the interests of efficiency and competitiveness. In this example, the wage bill has kept pace with productivity, negating the potential gains.

Activity 23
on page 43

Staff	Interviews conducted per day						
	Monday	**Tuesday**	**Wednesday**	**Thursday**	**Friday**	**Total**	**Average**
Dela	45	43	44	21	46	199	39.8
Corinne	54	50	51	55	53	263	52.6
David	38	41	40	44	39	202	40.4

Activity 24
on page 44

Staff	Interviews conducted per day						
	Monday	**Tuesday**	**Wednesday**	**Thursday**	**Friday**	**Total**	**Average**
Dela							
Actual	45.0	43.0	44.0	21.0	46.0	199.0	39.8
Target	52.5	52.5	52.5	52.5	52.5	262.5	52.5
% of target	85.7%	81.9%	83.8%	40.0%	87.6%	n/a	75.8%
Corinne							
Actual	54.0	50.0	51.0	55.0	53.0	263.0	52.6
Target	52.5	52.5	52.5	52.5	52.5	262.5	52.5
% of target	102.9%	95.2%	97.1%	104.8%	101.0%	n/a	100.2%
David							
Actual	38.0	41.0	40.0	44.0	39.0	202.0	40.4
Target	38.0	38.0	38.0	38.0	38.0	190.0	38.0
% of target	100.0%	107.9%	105.3%	115.8%	102.6%	n/a	106.3%

Activity 26 on page 46

	Answer	Spreadsheet formulae
Mean	236	= AVERAGE(A1:A9)
Median	249	= MEDIAN(A1:A9)
Mode	263	= MODE(A1:A9)

Not all formulae are as obvious as this, but many are.

Activity 32 on page 58

	A	B	C	D	E	F	G Spring	H Summer	I Autumn	J Winter
1							Spring	Summer	Autumn	Winter
2	2000	Spring	5100							
3		Summer	2900							
4		Autumn	7600		=AVERAGE(D5:D6)	=E4/4			=C4-F4	
5		Winter	4600	=SUM(C2:C5)	=AVERAGE(D6:D7)	=E5/4				=C5-F5
6	2001	Spring	5300	=SUM(C3:C6)	=AVERAGE(D7:D8)	=E6/4	=C6-F6			
7		Summer	3600	=SUM(C4:C7)	=AVERAGE(D8:D9)	=E7/4		=C7-F7		
8		Autumn	7500	=SUM(C5:C8)	=AVERAGE(D9:D10)	=E8/4			=C8-F8	
9		Winter	4300	=SUM(C6:C9)	=AVERAGE(D10:D11)	=E9/4				=C9-F9
10	2002	Spring	4900	=SUM(C7:C10)	=AVERAGE(D11:D12)	=E10/4	=C10-F10			
11		Summer	3900	=SUM(C8:C11)	=AVERAGE(D12:D13)	=E11/4		=C11-F11		
12		Autumn	7800	=SUM(C9:C12)	=AVERAGE(D13:D14)	=E12/4			=C12-F12	
13		Winter	5200	=SUM(C10:C13)	=AVERAGE(D14:D15)	=E13/4				=C13-F13
14	2003	Spring	5400	=SUM(C11:C14)	=AVERAGE(D15:D16)	=E14/4	=C14-F14			
15		Summer	3800	=SUM(C12:C15)	=AVERAGE(D16:D17)	=E15/4		=C15-F15		
16		Autumn	8500	=SUM(C13:C16)						
17		Winter	4900	=SUM(C14:C17)						
18							=SUM(G2:G17)	=SUM(H2:H17)	=SUM(I2:I17)	=SUM(J2:J17)
19										
20							=AVERAGE(G2:G17)	=AVERAGE(H2:H17)	=AVERAGE(I2:I17)	=AVERAGE(J2:J17)
21	2004	Total	23000				=$C$21/4	=$C$21/4	=$C$21/4	=$C$21/4
22							=SUM(G20:G21)	=SUM(H20:H21)	=SUM(I20:I21)	=SUM(J20:J21)
23										
24										
25										

If sales demand is 28,000 units the sales pattern will be as follows.

Spring	**Summer**	**Autumn**	**Winter**
6,837.5	5,354.17	9,395.83	6,412.5

Activity 38 on page 67

The information is organized in ascending order of employee number.

It could be organized in alphabetical order of last name or first name, by position, in chronological order of date joined, or (if the dates in the last column are recognized as dates) according to date of 2004 Annual Review.

The best way to organize the data is probably by last name. Arguably it could be organized by date of Annual Review, since this would highlight the fact that some reviews are overdue and action is needed.

Activity 40 on page 70

Cross-references to paragraph numbers involve less work and carry less risk of error. When you add material to a document, or delete material, all the subsequent page numbers are likely to change, so if you cross-refer to page numbers you will have to revise all the cross-references that appear after the insertion or deletion. If you cross-refer to paragraph numbers, however, only a few references will change if you delete something or insert something new.

Activity 43
on page 80

Products A and B both suffer a dip in sales in May and October, and both show a significant rise in sales in July and from October to December.

Activity 44
on page 82

Products A and B show opposite behaviour in the first two months. Product A sales roughly double in February, but fall back slightly in March. Product B sales roughly halve in February and fall a bit further in March.

Activity 52
on page 100

Office packages typically have a variety of clip-art images that you can use to liven up your documents, reports or presentations, but take care with these: many are rather cartoon-like and if you use them too much or use them inappropriately your work may not be taken seriously.

Product photos and diagrams may well be available from the production department in your organization.

The Internet is a fabulous source of graphic images, but again care is needed. If you use an image found on the Internet it may be subject to copyright restrictions.

Activity 54
on page 104

Task B can only be started once task A is completed, and task D can only be started once task C is completed. Task C can be done more or less concurrently with task B.

The 'actual' bars show that task A took longer than expected, making the start of tasks B and C late. Tasks B and C appear to have been done in the allotted time, but task D has not yet been started. It should have started at the beginning of week 3, but it will not be started until the end of that week.

6 Answers to the quick quiz

Answer 1   Top management usually want bottom-line or summary information about key areas. Lower down the organization, managers are interested in operational (day-to-day) details and information about individual staff performance, productivity and so on.

Answer 2   Collecting more and more information can result in diminishing returns because the cost of collection and the time needed to process and interpret the information begin to outweigh its extra value.

Answer 3   The first thing to do is to make a list of the items of information you have before you, perhaps numbering or coding them in some way.

Answer 4   ■ Inventory models, used for determining stock levels and re-order amounts.
■ Resource allocation models, to decide how to use up staff time, materials and so on in the most profitable way.
■ Budget models such as cash budgets and breakeven analysis.
■ Queuing models, which attempt to optimize customer waiting time, for example in a call centre or a supermarket.
■ Business plan models, used for overall planning by senior managers.

Answer 5   We were trying to tempt you to write about Gantt charts, so well done if you realized that we were actually referring to the use of limiting factors. This technique involves identifying the limiting factor(s), calculating the profit earned by each product per unit of the scarce resource, and then devising a plan that concentrates on the most profitable product first and then allocates any resources left over to other products.

Answer 6   Raw data means any data that has not been processed so as to turn it into useable information.

Answer 7   In 2002 the ratio was approximately 1:157. In 2003 it was approximately 1:168.

Answer 8   The mean can easily be distorted by the inclusion of one or more untypical figures, in other words a figure much higher or lower than the majority of the values.

Answer 9   To calculate the average when you have grouped data, you need to decide which value best represents all of the values in a particular class interval. It is a convention in statistics to take the mid-point of each class interval, on the assumption that the frequencies occur pretty evenly. In this example the midpoint is 22.

Answer 10   ■ Sixty-eight per cent of the values in a set of numbers will be within plus or minus **one standard deviation** of the arithmetic mean.
■ Ninety-five per cent of the values in a set of numbers will be within plus or minus **two standard deviations** of the mean.

Answer 11   There should be a 'hierarchy' of headings: an overall title, section headings and within each section up to three levels of sub-heading. Sections might be lettered A, B and so on; main points numbered 1, 2, and so on, paragraphs numbered 1.1, 1.2, 2.1, 2.2; and sub-paragraphs 1.2.1, and so on.

Answer 12 Numbers should be right-aligned and they are easier to read if you use the comma separator for thousands. Decimal points should line up, either by using a decimal tab or by adding extra zeros. A total figure is often advisable at the bottom of each column of figures and possibly at the end of each row.

Answer 13 The bars should be the same width.

Answer 14 A chart can be edited and formatted by right clicking on the chart as a whole or on an individual item within it and choosing from the menu options presented (Format chart, Format axis, etc.).

Answer 15 Pictograms present data in a simple and appealing way and for this reason they are often used in the media. However, pictograms are not appropriate if you need to give precise figures. You can use portions of a symbol to represent smaller quantities, but there are limits to what you can do.

7 Certificate

Completion of this certificate by an authorized person shows that you have worked through all the parts of this workbook and satisfactorily completed the assessments. The certificate provides a record of what you have done that may be used for exemptions or as evidence of prior learning against other nationally certificated qualifications.

Pergamon Flexible Learning and ILM are always keen to refine and improve their products. One of the key sources of information to help this process are people who have just used the product. If you have any information or views, good or bad, please pass these on.

INSTITUTE OF LEADERSHIP & MANAGEMENT

SUPERSERIES

Information in Management

....

has satisfactorily completed this workbook

Name of signatory ....

Position ....

Signature ....

Date ....

Official stamp

Fourth Edition

INSTITUTE OF LEADERSHIP & MANAGEMENT
SUPERSERIES
FOURTH EDITION

Achieving Quality	0 7506 5874 6
Appraising Performance	0 7506 5838 X
Becoming More Effective	0 7506 5887 8
Budgeting for Better Performance	0 7506 5880 0
Caring for the Customer	0 7506 5840 1
Collecting Information	0 7506 5888 6
Commitment to Equality	0 7506 5893 2
Controlling Costs	0 7506 5842 8
Controlling Physical Resources	0 7506 5886 X
Delegating Effectively	0 7506 5816 9
Delivering Training	0 7506 5870 3
Effective Meetings at Work	0 7506 5882 7
Improving Efficiency	0 7506 5871 1
Information in Management	0 7506 5890 8
Leading Your Team	0 7506 5839 8
Making a Financial Case	0 7506 5892 4
Making Communication Work	0 7506 5875 4
Managing Change	0 7506 5879 7
Managing Lawfully – Health, Safety and Environment	0 7506 5841 X
Managing Lawfully – People and Employment	0 7506 5853 3
Managing Relationships at Work	0 7506 5891 6
Managing Time	0 7506 5877 0
Managing Tough Times	0 7506 5817 7
Marketing and Selling	0 7506 5837 1
Motivating People	0 7506 5836 3
Networking and Sharing Information	0 7506 5885 1
Organizational Culture and Context	0 7506 5884 3
Organizational Environment	0 7506 5889 4
Planning and Controlling Work	0 7506 5813 4
Planning Training and Development	0 7506 5860 6
Preventing Accidents	0 7506 5835 5
Project and Report Writing	0 7506 5876 2
Securing the Right People	0 7506 5822 3
Solving Problems	0 7506 5818 5
Storing and Retrieving Information	0 7506 5894 0
Understanding Change	0 7506 5878 9
Understanding Finance	0 7506 5815 0
Understanding Quality	0 7506 5881 9
Working In Teams	0 7506 5814 2
Writing Effectively	0 7506 5883 5

To order – phone us direct for prices and availability details
(please quote ISBNs when ordering) on 01865 888190